A well-seasoned kitchen

Shrimp Tostada page 155

A well-seasoned kitchen

CLASSIC RECIPES FOR CONTEMPORARY LIVING

By mother and daughter, Sally Clayton and Lee Clayton Roper

To Christine —
Enjoy!
Lee Roper

Photography by Laurie Smith • Food styling by Erica McNeish

MLC Publishing, LLC
Denver, Colorado

Published in the United States by MLC Publishing, LLC, P.O. Box 6374, Denver, Colorado 80206.

All rights in and to the trademark "A Well-Seasoned Kitchen" are claimed exclusively by the publisher. No claims with
respect to any other brand name or mark used in this book are made; such names and marks are used for reference
purposes only, they are and remain the property of their respective owners and no endorsement or affiliation is
expressed or implied.

Publishers Cataloging-in-Publication Data
Clayton, Sally Elizabeth.
A well-seasoned kitchen: classic recipes for contemporary living/by mother and daughter, Sally Clayton and Lee Clayton
Roper; photography by Laurie Smith; food styling by Erica McNeish.—1st ed.—Denver, Colo.: MLC Pub., c2009.
p.; cm.
ISBN: 978-0-9841163-3-1
Includes index.
1. Cookery, American. 2. Menus. 3. Dinners and dining. 4. Entertaining. 5. Make-ahead cookery. I. Roper, Lee Clayton.
II. Smith, Laurie. III. McNeish, Erica. IV. title.
TX715 .C622 2009   2009933513
641.5/973—dc22   0910

Library of Congress Control Number: 2009933513

Printed in Singapore.

Printed on acid-free paper.

10 9 8 7 6 5 4 3 2 1
First edition

Food Styling: Erica McNeish
Design and art direction: Connie Robertson

www.seasonedkitchen.com

In all recipes unless otherwise noted,
• Dried herbs can be substituted for fresh, with 1 teaspoon dried = 1 tablespoon chopped fresh.
• Butter refers to salted butter.
• Onion refers to yellow onion.

dedication

This book is offered in heartfelt tribute to my late mother, Sally Clayton,

whose natural grace, remarkable style and strength serve as inspiration for this book

and for my life. It is also written in honor of my late father, Dr. Mack L. Clayton,

whose love and encouragement made me believe

I could do anything, including write and publish a cookbook.

Sausage and Spinach Torte page 137

contents

Cannellini Bean Dip with Truffle Oil **page 24**

thanks

A well-seasoned kitchen holds great meaning for me and represents more than a collection of recipes. It embodies a multitude of memories and underscores the deep bonds our family forged over shared meals and gatherings. I am indebted to many people who supported me on this deeply personal and fulfilling journey. I am grateful to the incredibly talented photographer, Laurie Smith, whose style captured the essence of every recipe; her partner, food stylist Erica McNeish, for her extraordinary ability to dress a plate and make every recipe look delicious; and their efficient assistant, Melanie Lenci, who ensured no detail was overlooked. Connie Robertson is the most innovative and talented designer with whom I've had the pleasure of working. She brought a special touch to this book by infusing my mother's point of view, despite never having met her. Karen Roehl, Cynthia Croasdaile, and Amy Hall worked diligently behind the scenes to get the book ready for print. I would have been lost without Sarah Eder, who brought amazing vision, creativity and communication skills to the effort. I owe my gratitude to good friends Evie and Paul Maxwell, who helped with the crucial task of finalizing the name of my book. I also thank my good friends Deborah Shaw and Laurie Wert, my brother Jim Clayton and my sister-in-law Carol Roper—all of whom made excellent models for several of the photos. Thanks to friends and family who, throughout the years, shared recipes and inspiration and were a constant source of support—there are too many to name, but you know who you are! Two people are above all responsible for inspiring me to take this book from vision to reality. First, Mom, whose style of cooking and entertaining gave me a lifelong love of bringing food, family and friends together. She encouraged and guided me, even after she was gone. And, of course, I thank my wonderful husband, Robert, my love, my constant supporter and my best food tester, without whom I never would have completed this project.

—Lee Clayton Roper, Denver, Colorado

Christmas Morning Eggs **page 34**

introduction

From my earliest memories, cooking and entertaining were an integral part of life in the Clayton household. In fact, Mom and Dad held weekly dinner parties to connect with friends and loved ones. Family and friends are very important to all of us; food is a way to bring everyone together. Mom and Dad created an environment that made everyone feel comfortable and enjoy themselves. Dad often spontaneously brought guests home knowing there would always be welcoming seats at the table. It was never a problem for Mom; she had an almost magical ability to stretch meals to feed what seemed to be an infinite number of people. Her love of cooking and entertaining became mine as well, and I held my first dinner party with my friend Lizzie Valentine, at age 16.

In developing this cookbook, Mom and I concentrated on the type of dishes we like best—simple and delicious recipes for everyday and easy entertaining. Mom didn't like to spend lots of time in the kitchen, and neither do I. We both much prefer to be among the company of others. In the pursuit of having our cake and eating it, too, we spent years collecting recipes that are at once easy, beautiful and scrumptious. You'll also find a couple of recipes where we broke a few of our own rules, and more preparation is needed. We loved them so much we decided to include them for those special occasions that warrant the extra effort.

In addition to individual recipes, we've also included several menu suggestions. Friends often tell me that menu creation is the most stressful aspect of entertaining. To help with this, we've featured several of our traditional family menus along with some tried-and-true favorites that I've served with success.

Finally, we focused on recipes that are as appealing to the eye as they are to the taste buds. Our beautiful feature photos were shot in natural light without any doctoring. When you make these recipes at home, you should feel confident that you'll have your own stunning results.

appetizers

Benedictine Cheese Canapés page 14

An appetizer is more than a small bite. It's a promise of what's to come at dinner and sets the stage for the evening. For as long as I can remember, my family has enjoyed appetizers—and we made a ritual of it. Dad would prepare an evening cocktail for Mom and himself (and for me and my brother, Jim, when we were old enough!) just before dinner. Mom would have an appetizer ready for us to enjoy. My husband, Robert, and I continue this tradition today. Both of us find comfort in having a cocktail or glass of wine paired with an easy appetizer after a busy day. When we have guests, I tend to prepare two or more to present a variety, and I make sure that they complement the rest of the meal.

Benedictine Cheese Canapés

SERVES 8 TO 10

Mom was raised in Louisville, Kentucky, and as a result, Derby Day is a major holiday for our family! We partake of all the traditional Kentucky items including Kentucky Corn Pudding, Country Ham, Derby Pie and, of course, Genuine Derby Day Mint Juleps. This recipe for Benedictine Cheese Canapés is a favorite in our house for the event. Mom insisted on using the food coloring for the pale green color for an authentic presentation. I added the tomato which pairs nicely with the cheese flavor. *(Photo, page 12)*

1 loaf thinly sliced white bread (such as Pepperidge Farm)
1 large cucumber
8 ounces cream cheese at room temperature
1 tablespoon grated onion
1 tablespoon mayonnaise
¼ teaspoon salt (or more to taste)
Dash cayenne pepper (to taste)
Dash green food coloring
Dash sugar (only if needed)
1 pint cherry tomatoes
Cayenne pepper

Preheat oven to 350 degrees.

Cut rounds out of each slice of bread (not using crusts) to desired size (we like 1- or 1 1/2-inch rounds). Place on a cookie sheet and bake for around 7 minutes until lightly toasted.

Peel, seed and grate the cucumber. Wrap in paper towel and squeeze/wring out as much moisture as possible. Combine with cream cheese (cut into slices), onion, mayonnaise, salt and cayenne pepper in a food processor and mix until well blended. Taste and adjust salt and cayenne pepper as needed. Stir in food coloring. Place in a dish, cover and refrigerate for several hours to let flavors blend.

Taste again, adjust salt and cayenne as needed. If cucumbers are bitter (some can be, especially if they are young), add a dash of sugar.

Top each toast round with some of the spread. Garnish with a slice of cherry tomato and lightly sprinkle with cayenne pepper.

MAKE AHEAD Toast rounds and cheese can be made earlier in the day. Place the cooled toast rounds in a ziploc baggie and store at room temperature; cover the cheese and store it in the refrigerator until ready to use.

Cheddar Chutney Tarts

MAKES AROUND 5 DOZEN

•

These tarts are small, but the size is perfect because they make rich and savory bites. Note that you will need to start ahead as the tarts require freezing before being baked.

8 ounces cream cheese at room
   temperature
1 cup grated sharp Cheddar cheese
½ teaspoon chopped garlic
1 teaspoon curry powder
⅓ cup mango chutney
4 medium green onions, chopped
Dash cayenne pepper
Dash Worcestershire sauce
1 package (17 ounces) frozen puff
   pastry, thawed (2 sheets)

Using an electric mixer with a whisk attachment, mix the cream cheese until smooth. Add the Cheddar, garlic and curry powder and blend well. Chop up the large pieces in the chutney and add to the cheese mixture along with onions, cayenne pepper and Worcestershire sauce. Mix well. Season to taste with salt. Set aside.

On a lightly floured surface roll out one piece of puff pastry into a 12-inch square. Cut into 2-inch squares. Press into small mini-muffin tins and prick with a fork. Repeat with second pastry sheet. Spoon 1 teaspoon filling into center of each square. (You are likely to have a few squares of pastry left over.) Freeze tarts in the tins.

To bake the tarts, preheat the oven to 400 degrees. Bake frozen tarts 15 minutes until pastry is golden. Serve hot.

MAKE AHEAD Tarts can be kept frozen for up to 6 months. The filling can be made up to 3 days ahead, covered and refrigerated. Bring to room temperature before using; then proceed with freezing before baking.

NOTE If you aren't baking tarts the same day, once they are frozen, remove them from the muffin tins and place in freezer bags to store. Place tarts back into mini-muffin tins to bake.

Spicy Chicken on Pita Triangles

SERVES 12+

This recipe has long been a staple at my cocktail parties and it is always a favorite. The recipe makes a lot, but the extra chicken mixture freezes well and can be saved for another party!

2 chicken breast halves, cooked and finely chopped
12 ounces cream cheese at room temperature
1½ cups shredded sharp Cheddar cheese (around 6 ounces)
¼ cup sour cream
¼ cup finely chopped red onion
3 green onions, finely chopped
1 to 2 tablespoons chopped pickled jalapeño peppers (or more to taste)
1 teaspoon ground cumin
1 teaspoon chili powder
½ teaspoon ground coriander
1 teaspoon chopped garlic
4 pitas split into 2 rounds each
Sliced ripe olives

Preheat oven to 375 degrees.

In a large mixing bowl, combine the chicken, cream cheese, Cheddar, sour cream, red onion, green onion, jalapeño peppers, cumin, chili powder, coriander and garlic. Stir until well mixed, then season with salt and pepper to taste. Spread 1/8 of mixture on each pita round. Cut each round into 8 triangle pieces. Place on a baking sheet and bake for 5 to 7 minutes or until bubbly and hot. Garnish with ripe olive slices.

MAKE AHEAD The chicken mixture can be frozen for up to 3 months. Thaw in the refrigerator, then bring to room temperature—if the mixture is too cold it won't spread well.

Toasted Clam Rolls

SERVES 12

Mother made these rolls for years, and she was keen on including the recipe in this cookbook. Before making the final cut, I was sure to try them with friends, who gobbled them up and insisted I make more. Mother knows best!

3 cans (6½ ounce) minced (not chopped) clams

⅓ cup chopped green onion

½ cup mayonnaise

6 tablespoons freshly grated Parmesan cheese (or more to taste)

1 teaspoon Worcestershire sauce

¾ teaspoon garlic powder

¼ to ½ teaspoon Tabasco sauce

1 loaf (16 ounce) thin-sliced sandwich bread (Pepperidge Farm works great)

4 tablespoons butter, melted

Preheat oven to 425 degrees. Place rack in upper third of oven. Grease a large baking sheet.

Drain clams well and combine with onion, mayonnaise, cheese, Worcestershire sauce, garlic powder and Tabasco.

Trim crusts from bread and roll each slice with a rolling pin until very thin. Spread about 1 tablespoon of the clam mixture onto each slice of bread—to the edge on three sides and to within 1/8 inch of one of the shorter sides. Starting with the opposite short side, roll up. Brush well with the melted butter and cut in half. Place rolls seam-side down on the prepared baking sheet. Bake in the upper third of the oven for 12 minutes or until lightly browned. Note that they are likely to brown faster on the bottom, so watch carefully! Serve warm.

MAKE AHEAD Make rolls, omitting butter but still cut in half. Place on cookie sheet and freeze. When frozen, place in a plastic bag, seal, and return to freezer. To serve, place frozen rolls on a greased baking sheet, bring to room temperature, and then brush with melted butter before baking.

Smoked Salmon on Mini Cheddar-Dill Scones

MAKES 45 TO 50 SMALL SCONES

●

These scones are easy to make and don't take much time at all. Stuff them with smoked salmon or slices of ham and honey mustard as an alternative. Or, make the scones larger and serve them with your favorite soup.

SCONES
2 large eggs
½ cup milk
2 tablespoons chopped fresh dill
2 cups flour
1 tablespoon baking powder
1 teaspoon salt
½ teaspoon ground pepper
7 tablespoons cold unsalted butter, divided
1½ cups grated sharp Cheddar cheese

FILLING
Smoked salmon pieces
Sprigs of dill
Lemon zest pieces

Preheat oven to 425 degrees. Place rack in upper third of oven.

In a small mixing bowl, whisk together eggs and milk until well blended. Whisk in dill and set aside.

Place flour, baking powder, salt, and pepper in the bowl of a food processor. Process to mix. Cut 6 tablespoons of the butter into pieces, add to flour mixture and pulse just until butter is incorporated. Add the grated cheese and pulse one or two times to blend. While the machine is running, quickly add milk mixture through the feed tube and process the dough just until moist clumps begin to form a ball.

Turn dough out onto a lightly floured surface and shape into a ball. Using your fingers, flatten dough to 1/2-inch thickness. (Do not make thinner as the scones won't rise.) Cut out mini scones with a 1-inch round cutter and place on a nonstick baking sheet. Reroll scraps and continue cutting. Melt remaining 1 tablespoon of butter and brush over top of each scone. Bake in the upper third of the oven for 12 to 15 minutes or until golden brown.

Let cool, then slice in half. Place a piece of salmon, sprig of dill and piece of lemon zest inside each scone. Serve immediately.

MAKE AHEAD The mini scones can be made ahead and stored in an airtight container at room temperature for up to 24 hours. They can also be frozen for up to 3 months.

VARIATION Cut the scones out larger (about the size of a biscuit) and serve them with a hot soup or stew.

Smoked Salmon and Goat Cheese Torte

SERVES 12

●

The combination of goat cheese, cream cheese and salmon is always a winner. Pistachios add color and an interesting flavor to the mix.

6 ounces mild goat cheese at room temperature
6 ounces cream cheese at room temperature
Ground white pepper to taste
½ cup smoked salmon, scraps or minced (2 ounces)
¼ cup pistachios, lightly toasted, divided

Blend together the two cheeses and white pepper in a food processor until smooth.

Line a 3- or 4-cup deep bowl or fluted mold with plastic wrap. Spoon 1/3 of the cheese mixture into the mold, spread together, pack down and smooth the top with the back of the spoon. Sprinkle the salmon evenly over the top and press down with the spoon. Spoon another 1/3 of the cheese mixture on top of the salmon, spread together, pack down, and smooth the top.

Set aside 1 tablespoon of the chopped pistachios and sprinkle the rest on top of the cheese; press it down with the back of a spoon. Spoon the last 1/3 of the cheese mixture over the nuts, spread together, pack down and smooth the top with a spatula.

Cover with the overlapping plastic wrap and chill for at least 2 hours. One hour before serving, uncover the top, turn the mold upside down and unmold onto a large plate. Remove the plastic wrap and sprinkle the reserved chopped pistachios over the top. Serve with crackers or crostini.

MAKE AHEAD Torte can be made up to 24 hours in advance and stored, covered, in the refrigerator.

Sally's Smoked Trout Paté

SERVES 6

In a household with three fly fishermen—Dad, my brother Jim and me—there was always an abundance of trout (this was in the days before catch and release). Mom was always looking for interesting ways to fix it, and created this recipe—she even smoked the trout herself. It is still a family favorite although today we tend to make it with purchased smoked trout.

2 cups loosely packed, flaked smoked rainbow or brown trout, skin removed (around 10 to 12 ounces)

½ cup butter at room temperature

4 ounces cream cheese at room temperature

3 tablespoons heavy cream (use half and half as a substitute)

2 tablespoons freshly squeezed lemon juice (or more to taste)

Mix all ingredients together in a blender or food processor. Season with salt and pepper (careful with the salt—you don't need much due to the smoky flavor).

Cover and chill. Bring to room temperature for at least 15 minutes before serving. For a nice presentation, pack it into a pretty serving bowl or mound it in the middle of a small serving platter. Serve with crackers.

MAKE AHEAD Paté can be made 2 to 3 days ahead, covered and stored in the refrigerator. Can also be frozen.

Camembert Sauté

SERVES 6 TO 8

●

A simple and delicious appetizer that is always a hit! Be sure not to let the butter get too hot as you can easily burn the bread crumbs.

1 4- to 6-inch round Camembert cheese (can also use Brie)
1 egg, beaten
1 cup fresh bread crumbs
4 tablespoons unsalted butter, divided
1/2 cup chopped green onion

Dip the cheese in the egg and then coat all sides with the bread crumbs.

Heat 2 tablespoons of the butter in a small skillet over medium heat just until it starts to brown. Brown cheese on all sides. Remove to a serving plate and keep warm.

Wipe out the skillet with a paper towel and add the remaining butter to the skillet. Melt over medium heat and when foamy, sauté the onions for 2 minutes. Sprinkle sautéed onions over the cheese round and serve immediately with crackers.

Cannellini Bean Dip with Truffle Oil

If you're a fan of truffle oil, you will love this dish. And, if you aren't, you will be a convert after one scoop of this dip! If you don't have lemon-flavored olive oil, use regular, but increase the amount of lemon juice a bit. *(Photo, page 8)*

2 cans (15 ounce) cannellini (or Great Northern) beans, drained and rinsed

⅔ cup lemon-flavored olive oil

1½ to 2 teaspoons minced garlic

¼ cup freshly squeezed lemon juice

½ cup Italian parsley leaves, stems removed

2 tablespoons white truffle oil

Blend drained and rinsed beans, olive oil, garlic, lemon juice and parsley in a food processor until well blended but still slightly chunky. Season with salt and pepper to taste. Just before serving, swirl in truffle oil (don't completely mix in). Delicious served with pita chips.

MAKE AHEAD The bean dip can be made, without adding the truffle oil, earlier in the day, covered and stored in the refrigerator. Bring to room temperature and swirl in truffle oil.

Santo's Cheese Spread

SERVES 12

When I was growing up, my best friend Katey's family spent spring break at her grandmother's house in Palm Desert, California. A local restaurant there called Santo's sold the most fabulous cheese spread. Lucky for us, the Hartwells would always bring the treat home to Denver. Sadly, the restaurant closed before we could get the recipe. After many hours in the kitchen trying to duplicate it, Katey's mother and I actually found a recipe that, with a few adjustments, comes close to the Santo's original.

¼ cup unsalted butter at room temperature
8 ounces cream cheese at room temperature
8 ounces Kaukauna Club sharp Cheddar cheese
3 tablespoons dry sherry
1½ tablespoons dry vermouth
⅜ teaspoon dry mustard
¼ teaspoon Lowry's seasoned salt
⅜ teaspoon celery salt
½ teaspoon Worcestershire sauce
¼ teaspoon dried oregano

Blend butter, cream cheese and Cheddar in a food processor until well blended. (Alternatively, slightly soften the butter and cream cheese in the microwave and then stir by hand.) Stir in sherry, vermouth, mustard, salts, Worcestershire sauce and oregano until well mixed. Cover and refrigerate for several hours. Serve with crackers and celery.

MAKE AHEAD Spread can be made up to 1 day ahead, covered and refrigerated.

Melted Gruyère and Bacon Dip

SERVES 8

You can't go wrong with melted cheese and crispy fried bacon. No matter how much you make of this crowd pleaser, there will never be any left over!

8 slices bacon
8 ounces cream cheese at room temperature
½ cup mayonnaise
1 cup shredded Gruyère (or Swiss) cheese
2 tablespoons finely chopped green onions
½ sleeve Ritz crackers
3 tablespoons butter, melted

Preheat the oven to 350 degrees.

Cook the bacon until crisp; break into crumbles.

Mix together the cream cheese, mayonnaise and Gruyère cheese. Stir in the green onions and bacon. Spread evenly in a shallow baking dish.

Crush the crackers and mix together with the butter. Sprinkle on top of cheese and bacon mixture. Bake for 20 to 25 minutes or until hot. Serve with crackers.

MAKE AHEAD Dip can be assembled but not baked earlier in the day, covered with plastic wrap and refrigerated. Bring to room temperature before baking.

A well-seasoned memory

Our family has long held Steamboat Springs, Colorado as a special place in our hearts. One particular time in Steamboat when I was a teenager, I called home around dinnertime and asked Mom if I could bring along five hungry friends. Without hesitation, Mom agreed. As was typical, she managed to easily stretch a family dinner to feed five more with no effort. Mom's creativity and ability to make any meal work was nothing short of miraculous!

Sally with her husband, Mack, relaxing after a day of skiing.

Pesto Cheese Wafers

MAKES UP TO 4 DOZEN

To make planning simple, this dough can be made ahead and frozen for several months. We always love to have a few appetizers in the freezer, either for last minute guests or to make our next cocktail party easier.

1½ cups grated Cheddar cheese
½ cup butter at room temperature
1 cup flour
¼ teaspoon cayenne pepper
⅛ teaspoon white pepper
1 cup fresh basil leaves
½ cup pine nuts
½ cup grated Parmesan cheese
½ teaspoon garlic

Preheat the oven to 350 degrees. Combine the Cheddar, butter, flour and peppers in the bowl of a food processor and mix until well blended. Transfer to another container. In the bowl of the food processor place the basil, pine nuts, Parmesan cheese and garlic and process until well mixed. Add the cheese mixture and pulse a few times to blend well.

Shape dough into 2 logs. Wrap in plastic wrap and refrigerate for several hours or until firm. Cut into 1/4-inch slices. Place side of large cutting knife blade over the top of each slice, and push down with your hand on the blade to flatten each slice to around 1/8-inch thick. Place slices on parchment-lined baking sheet. Bake for 10 to 12 minutes or until edges are golden brown. Can be served warm or at room temperature.

MAKE AHEAD Dough can be made up to chilling point, wrapped and frozen for up to three months. Thaw in the refrigerator before baking.

Spicy Pecans

Not only are these nuts delicious for everyday, they make an excellent hostess gift. Package them in a festive container and give them as an alternative to the standard bottle of wine.

4 tablespoons butter
1 tablespoon Worcestershire sauce
2 teaspoons Tabasco sauce
1 tablespoon salad seasoning
    such as McCormick's Salad
    Supreme Seasoning
1 teaspoon salt
½ teaspoon garlic salt
¼ teaspoon pepper
1 pound pecan halves

In a large skillet, melt the butter over low heat. Add spices and stir until well blended. Add nuts and toss to coat well. Cover and cook over low heat for 20 to 25 minutes, stirring occasionally, until hot and lightly toasted. Drain in a single layer on a brown paper bag (a cut grocery bag laid flat works well). Store in an airtight container.

MAKE AHEAD Cooked pecans can be stored in an airtight container at room temperature for up to one week.

Lee's Favorite Cosmos

●

This recipe makes the best Cosmopolitan I've ever had, and many of my friends agree! Fresh lime juice is the key. *(Photo, page 31)*

3½ tablespoons (1¾ ounces) really good vodka
2 tablespoons (1 ounce) Cointreau
2 tablespoons (1 ounce) cranberry juice
1 tablespoon (½ ounce) freshly squeezed lime juice (no substitutes!)

Chill martini glasses quickly by filling them with ice water and letting them sit for a minute. Drain and dry.

Fill a martini shaker with ice. Add all ingredients. Shake well. Pour through a cocktail strainer into a chilled martini glass.

Perfect Sidecar

●

Friends Joan Perlow and Deborah Shaw love to drink Sidecars but are quite particular about how they're made. Rather than having Joan give the exact recipe to the bartender every time she wants one, her clever husband David had business cards printed with the exact recipe. Joan and Deborah both carry their cocktail cards in their purses at all times to ensure they get the Perfect Sidecar. *(Photo, page 31)*

3 parts sour mix
1 part brandy
1 part Cointreau

Fill a martini shaker with ice. Add all ingredients. Shake well. Pour through a cocktail strainer into martini glass with a sugared rim.

Genuine Derby Day Mint Juleps

SERVES 12+

For years, we've been in pursuit of the perfect Mint Julep to accompany our Derby Day festivities. We think this recipe is just right—not too much bourbon, not too sweet and just enough mint. Yum!

2 cups water

2 cups sugar

⅓ cup + ¼ cup packed fresh mint leaves, divided (plus sprigs for garnish)

1 bottle good bourbon (Mom preferred Jack Daniels)

Make a simple syrup by bringing the water to a boil. Remove from heat and stir in sugar. Continue to stir until sugar dissolves and the water is no longer cloudy (doesn't take very long). Stir in 1/3 cup mint, crushing the mint leaves with the spoon. Cover and allow to steep for several hours or overnight (the longer the better!).

Place a few mint leaves in the bottom of each mint julep cup, and crush with a muddler (or back of a spoon). Fill each cup with lots of ice (to the top). Add 3 ounces (1/3 cup) of bourbon, 3 to 4 tablespoons of the mint simple syrup (or more to taste) and a sprig of fresh mint. Enjoy!

NOTE The mint simple syrup will keep in the refrigerator for several months. It's great for mojitos, too!

Clockwise from bottom: Lee's Favorite Cosmo, Genuine Derby Day Mint Julep and Perfect Sidecar

breakfast and brunch

The biggest secret to entertaining is brunch. It is inexpensive and the easiest way to entertain. Even better, nearly everything can be made in advance. Many of my favorite recipes aren't just reserved for entertaining—they're a wonderful treat for any weekend morning, and who doesn't love a scrumptious breakfast?

Poached Eggs in Italian Tomato Sauce

SERVES 2 TO 4

●

These eggs are a quick and delicious treat even in the middle of the week.

2 tablespoons extra virgin olive oil

1 can (14 ounce) diced tomatoes with Italian herbs, undrained

¼ teaspoon chopped garlic

1 tablespoon chopped fresh parsley

1 teaspoon chopped fresh rosemary

4 large or extra large eggs

1 to 2 tablespoons grated Parmesan cheese

Heat the olive oil in a large nonstick skillet over medium heat. Add the tomatoes with their juice, garlic, parsley and rosemary. Bring to a boil, reduce heat to medium and boil for 3 to 4 minutes, softening the tomatoes and reducing the sauce a bit. Make four hollowed-out spaces and put one egg in each space. Cover and cook until eggs are done they way you like them.

Place eggs and sauce on plates, sprinkle with parmesan cheese, salt and pepper and serve.

Christmas Morning Eggs

SERVES 8

●

The Clayton family has been eating these eggs on Christmas morning since my brother Jim and I were little kids. I can't recall a Christmas morning without them! We usually serve them with country ham and sweet rolls, like Overnight Bundt Caramel Rolls. *(Photo, page 10)*

2 cups shredded sharp Cheddar cheese (or more to taste)

8 large eggs

1 cup canned chopped green chiles

1 cup sour cream

Preheat oven to 425 degrees. Generously butter 8 large ramekins or other individual baking dishes.

Spread 1/4 cup of cheese on the bottom of each prepared ramekin. Make a well in the middle and crack an egg into the well. Sprinkle 2 tablespoons of green chiles around the egg. Spoon 2 tablespoons of sour cream on top of the green chiles. Season to taste with salt and pepper. Place on a cookie sheet and bake for around 10 to 12 minutes or until the eggs are cooked to desired doneness (less time if you like your eggs runny, more if you like them well done). Let sit for a minute or two before serving—note that eggs continue to cook after being removed from the oven.

MAKE AHEAD Eggs can be prepared in the ramekins, covered and stored in the refrigerator overnight. Bring to room temperature before baking.

Sausage, Mushroom and Pepper Strata
SERVES 12

•

Several years ago, my friend Diane Heidel and I held a cookie exchange brunch. I had seen several different strata recipes that all looked good and couldn't decide which one to make, so I combined what I thought was the best in all of them and created this recipe. It was a big hit. I have served it several times since.

6 slices sourdough bread
  (small to medium sized)
⅔ package (5 ounce) garlic &
  cheese croutons
1 pound mild Italian turkey or
  chicken sausage
⅔ cup diced green bell pepper
⅔ cup diced red bell pepper
1 cup chopped green onion
  (a little less if strong)
2 cups grated sharp Cheddar
  cheese
3⅓ cups whole milk
12 ounces sliced fresh mushrooms
1½ teaspoon dry mustard
7 eggs
1 can (10¾ ounce) Cream of
  Mushroom Soup

Grease a 9x13-inch baking dish.

Cut sourdough bread into 1-inch cubes and spread in bottom of prepared pan. Mix in croutons. Set aside.

In a large skillet over medium high heat, brown sausage; drain. Chop briefly in a food processor to break into small pieces. Spread over bread cubes and crouton mixture. Sprinkle chopped green pepper, red pepper, and green onions evenly over sausage in pan. Top with Cheddar.

In a large mixing bowl, whisk together the eggs, milk, mushroom soup and dry mustard. Slowly pour over top of casserole, making sure to cover entire casserole evenly.

Sauté mushrooms in a non-stick skillet until cooked and water has evaporated. Spread over top of casserole. Cover and refrigerate overnight.

When ready to cook the strata, preheat the oven to 350 degrees.

Place the pan on the middle rack in the oven and bake for about an hour—it can hold in the oven for a while.

NOTE This recipe can easily be doubled or tripled for a large brunch. Great for the holidays with its red and green color from the peppers!

MAKE AHEAD The strata can be prepared, covered and refrigerated up to a day in advance before baking.

Deviled Eggs in Madras Sauce

SERVES 10 TO 12

●

This recipe is ideal as part of a brunch buffet. With a full menu, this dish will easily serve closer to 15 people. Start making this recipe the day before as the eggs need to chill overnight.

DEVILED EGGS
12 hard-boiled eggs
½ cup mayonnaise
1 tablespoon curry powder
(may need more)
1 tablespoon soy sauce
1 tablespoon finely chopped green
  onions
1 tablespoon finely chopped fresh
  parsley
1 teaspoon Dijon mustard
Cayenne pepper to taste

MADRAS SAUCE
¼ cup unsalted butter
¼ cup chopped onion
¼ cup peeled, cored, chopped apple
2½ tablespoons flour
1 tablespoon curry powder
  (may need more)
1 cup chicken broth
1 cup heavy cream
Lemon juice to taste*

*I typically use the juice from
half a large lemon.*

Butter a 9x13-inch baking dish (or any dish that will hold the egg halves in one layer).

Carefully remove the shells from the eggs; halve the eggs lengthwise and remove the yolks, reserving the whites. In a medium mixing bowl, mash the yolks with a fork and stir together with the mayonnaise, curry powder, soy sauce, green onions, parsley and Dijon mustard. Season to taste with salt and cayenne pepper. Adjust curry powder as needed. Spoon or pipe mixture into egg white halves. Place in prepared dish, cover and chill overnight.

Preheat oven to 350 degrees.

In a large saucepan over medium-low heat, melt the butter. Add the onion and apple and cook, stirring occasionally, for about 5 minutes or until the onion is softened. Stir in the flour and curry powder, reduce heat to low and continue cooking, stirring, for another 3 minutes. Stir in the broth and bring mixture to a boil. Reduce heat to low and simmer for 20 minutes. Stir in cream, again bring to a boil, reduce heat to low and cook for another 5 to 10 minutes or until the sauce thickens slightly. Remove from heat and add lemon juice, salt and pepper to taste. Adjust curry powder as needed.

Pour the sauce evenly over the eggs in the prepared dish and bake for 10 to 15 minutes or until the sauce is bubbly and hot. Serve immediately. Can be served with white or brown rice if you like, or just on its own.

Cinnamon Raisin Bread Custard with Fresh Berries

SERVES 12

●

I have made this recipe for years and it is always a big hit. Mom loved it, too. A good quality cinnamon raisin bread makes all the difference. *(Photo, page 32)*

8 slices good quality cinnamon raisin bread
½ cup butter, melted
4 eggs
2 egg yolks
¾ cup sugar
3 cups whole milk
1 cup whipping cream
1 tablespoon vanilla extract
3 cups mixed fresh berries (blueberries, blackberries, raspberries)
Powdered sugar

Brush both sides of the bread slices with the melted butter. Line a 9x13x2-inch glass baking dish with the buttered bread slices. Set aside.

In a large mixing bowl, whisk the eggs and egg yolks. Add the sugar, milk, cream and vanilla and whisk until well mixed. Slowly pour through a strainer over the top of the bread slices, covering them evenly and completely. If the bread slices float to the top of the egg mixture, gently push them down with your finger. Cover and refrigerate at least 2 hours or overnight.

If refrigerated all day or overnight, about 1 hour before baking take the dish out of the refrigerator to bring it to room temperature before proceeding.

Preheat oven to 350 degrees.

Place the baking dish on a large baking sheet with sides on the middle rack of your oven. Pour 2 cups hot water into the baking sheet (around the baking dish). Bake for 30 to 35 minutes or until the top is lightly browned and custard is cooked (it should spring back when you push lightly on the top). Cool slightly, sprinkle with fresh berry mixture and sift powdered sugar over the top. Cut into 12 pieces and serve.

NOTE Baking time should be increased 5 to 10 minutes if you do not use a glass dish.

MAKE AHEAD Can be assembled but not baked up to 24 hours in advance. Bring to room temperature before baking.

Shelburne Farms French Toast

SERVES 6 TO 8

●

Our friends the Lipsons gave us a stay at the Shelburne Farms Inn in Vermont as a wedding present. The food at this wonderful inn was absolutely delicious, especially the French toast. The chef was kind enough to share the recipe with me.

6 tablespoons crème fraiche
  (see Note)
6 teaspoons cinnamon, divided
¾ teaspoon ground nutmeg, divided
½ cup + 6 tablespoons maple
  syrup, divided
2 cups half and half
4 eggs
1 cup sliced almonds
1 cup crushed cornflakes
12+ slices cinnamon raisin bread
  (chef recommends O Bread
  from a Vermont bakery, but
  any good quality cinnamon
  raisin bread will do)
¼ cup butter, divided

In a small mixing bowl, stir together the crème fraiche, 1/2 teaspoon cinnamon, 1/2 teaspoon nutmeg and 6 tablespoons of the maple syrup. Set aside.

In a large mixing bowl, whisk together the half and half, eggs, and remaining cinnamon, nutmeg and maple syrup. In a shallow dish, mix together the sliced almonds and cornflakes. Dip each bread slice into the egg batter, then in the almond cornflake mixture. Heat 2 tablespoons butter over medium heat in a large skillet or griddle. Brown 4 bread slices on both sides until coating is cooked and toast is golden brown. Watch carefully as the cornflakes can burn. Remove and keep warm. Add 2 more tablespoons of butter to the skillet and continue until all slices have been cooked. Serve with crème fraiche mixture and real Vermont maple syrup on the side.

NOTE Crème fraiche is the French, slightly less sour version of sour cream. It is available at Whole Foods and specialty retail stores. If you can't find it in your area, substitute sour cream and add a bit of sugar to taste.

Sour Cream Peach Muffins

22 MUFFINS

Every fall, Mom used to buy peaches from her friend Dorothy Cameron, whose son grows them on Colorado's Western Slope. We're always on the lookout for good peach recipes and this one has become a favorite.

1½ cups light brown sugar, firmly packed
⅔ cup vegetable oil
1 egg, beaten
1 cup sour cream
1 teaspoon baking soda
1 teaspoon vanilla
1 teaspoon salt
2½ cups flour
1½ cups peeled, pitted and chopped fresh peaches
½ cup chopped pecans or almonds
Cinnamon sugar

Preheat oven to 325 degrees. Spray 18 muffin cups with nonstick cooking spray. (Fill empty cups halfway with water so the pan doesn't burn.)

Whisk together the sugar, oil and egg in a large mixing bowl, making sure the sugar doesn't stay in clumps. In a separate, small bowl, whisk together the sour cream, soda, vanilla and salt. Stir the sour cream mixture into the sugar mixture, and then stir in the flour just until incorporated—do not overmix. Fold in the peaches and nuts. With a large, spring-loaded ice cream scoop, place one scoop of batter into each muffin cup. Sprinkle the tops lightly with cinnamon sugar. Bake for 30 minutes, or until a tester inserted in the middle comes out clean. Let sit for a few minutes in the pan, and then remove from pan to a wire rack to cool. Best served warm.

VARIATION Can substitute cored, peeled and chopped fresh apples for the chopped peaches.

HIGH ALTITUDE No adjustments are necessary.

Pumpkin Cream Cheese Muffins

24 MUFFINS

●

A delicious morning treat, especially in the Fall.

8 ounces cream cheese at room
  temperature
4 eggs
2 cups sugar
2 cups cooked, puréed pumpkin
  (around one 15- or 16-ounce can)
1¼ cups vegetable oil
3 cups flour
3 teaspoons ground cinnamon
1½ teaspoons ground cloves
1½ teaspoons ground nutmeg
1 teaspoon ground ginger
Pinch cardamom
1 teaspoon salt
1 teaspoon baking soda
½ cup chopped pecans

Preheat oven to 350 degrees. Spray 24 muffin cups with nonstick cooking spray.

Place the cream cheese block between two pieces of wax paper and roll to slightly flatten, so that it is around 4 inches by 6 inches. Freeze.

In a large mixing bowl, whisk the eggs, then whisk in the sugar, pumpkin and vegetable oil. Set aside. In a medium mixing bowl, whisk together the flour, cinnamon, cloves, nutmeg, ginger, cardamom, salt and baking soda. Add to the egg mixture all at once and stir just until blended—do not overmix. Fill the muffin tins around 3/4 full (I like to use a large spring-loaded ice cream scoop).

Remove cream cheese from the freezer and cut into 24 1-inch squares. Push one square into the middle of each muffin. Sprinkle 1 teaspoon of chopped pecans over the top of each. Bake for 20 to 25 minutes or until a toothpick inserted into a muffin (not where the cream cheese is) comes out clean. Cool for 5 minutes in the pan; remove to a wire rack to cool completely. Note that the cream cheese will be very hot initially.

HIGH ALTITUDE Reduce the baking soda by 1/8 teaspoon, increase the vegetable oil by 2 tablespoons and use extra large eggs.

Blueberry Lemon Muffins

16 MUFFINS

The combination of lemon and blueberry always works well, and these muffins are no exception.

2 cups flour
1 cup sugar, divided
1 tablespoon baking powder
½ teaspoon salt
Zest from 1 lemon
1 egg
1 cup whole milk
¾ cup butter, melted and cooled slightly, divided
1 cup blueberries (fresh or frozen, but the latter must be thawed and drained)
2 tablespoons lemon juice

Preheat oven to 375 degrees. Spray 16 muffin cups with nonstick cooking spray. (Fill empty cups halfway with water so the pan doesn't burn.)

In a large mixing bowl, whisk together the flour, 1/2 cup of the sugar, baking powder, salt and lemon zest. Set aside.

In a medium mixing bowl, whisk the egg; whisk in the milk and 1/2 cup of the melted butter. Stir the egg mixture into the dry ingredients just until mixed (batter will be lumpy). Gently fold in blueberries. Fill muffin cups 2/3 full (I like to use a large spring-loaded ice cream scoop). Bake for 20 minutes or until a tester inserted in the center of one of the muffins comes out clean.

While the muffins are baking, make the topping: Combine the remaining 1/4 cup melted butter and the lemon juice. Put in a shallow dish. Put remaining 1/2 cup sugar in another shallow dish.

When the muffins are slightly cooled, remove from the pan and dunk the tops into the lemon-butter mixture, then into the sugar. Place on a wire rack to cool completely.

HIGH ALTITUDE No adjustments are necessary.

Very Lemony Bread

MAKES 1 LOAF

Delicious as part of a brunch menu or with a cup of tea!

1½ cups flour, sifted
1 teaspoon baking powder
1 teaspoon salt
⅓ cup butter, softened
1¼ cups sugar, divided
3 tablespoons lemon extract
   (a 1-ounce bottle)
2 eggs
½ cup milk
1½ tablespoons lemon zest
½ cup chopped pecans
¼ cup lemon juice

Preheat oven to 350 degrees. Grease and flour a 9x5-inch loaf pan.

In a medium mixing bowl, sift together the flour, baking powder and salt (you will have sifted the flour twice). Set aside.

With an electric mixer, beat the butter until light and fluffy, then add 1 cup of the sugar and lemon extract and continue beating until blended. With the motor running, add the eggs one at a time and continue beating until blended. Add 1/3 of the sifted flour mixture, alternating with 1/3 of the milk until all the flour and milk have been added. With a spatula or spoon, fold in the lemon zest and chopped pecans. Pour the batter into the prepared pan and bake for one hour, or until a tester inserted in the middle comes out clean.

While the bread is baking, whisk together the lemon juice and remaining 1/4 cup sugar. Let stand at room temperature while bread is baking.

Cool the bread in the pan for 15 minutes. Poke holes in the top with an ice pick or a fork and immediately drizzle the lemon mixture over the top. Let sit until lemon mixture is absorbed, around 5 minutes. Remove from pan and place on a wire rack to finish cooling.

NOTE This bread tastes best if you store it, wrapped in foil, for at least one day before serving.

HIGH ALTITUDE No adjustments are necessary.

Rhubarb Nut Bread

MAKES 1 OR 2 LOAVES

Mom loved rhubarb and always grew it in her garden. To make use of her harvest, she had several great recipes and this is one of them. Make this bread during the spring or summer when fresh rhubarb is plentiful.

⅔ cup vegetable oil
1 egg, lightly beaten
1½ cups packed light brown sugar
1 cup buttermilk
1 teaspoon baking soda
1 teaspoon salt
1 teaspoon vanilla
2½ cups flour
1½ cups diced peeled, raw rhubarb
   stalks
½ cup chopped pecans

Preheat oven to 325 degrees. Lightly butter one 9x5-inch or two 8x4-inch loaf pans.

In a large mixing bowl, whisk together the vegetable oil and egg, then stir in the brown sugar. In a small mixing bowl, stir together the buttermilk, baking soda, salt and vanilla. Stir 1/4 cup of the buttermilk mixture into the brown sugar mixture, then stir in 1/2 cup of the flour. Continue adding the buttermilk mixture, alternating with the flour, then stir in the last 1/2 cup of flour. Do not overmix. Fold in the diced rhubarb and chopped pecans.

Turn batter into one prepared loaf pan or divide it equally between two. Bake one pan for one hour and two pans for 45 minutes or until a toothpick inserted in the middle comes out clean. Cool bread in the pan on racks for 10 to 15 minutes, then remove and place on wire rack to cool completely.

NOTE Use only the stalks of rhubarb, never the leaves as they are poisonous.

HIGH ALTITUDE No adjustments are necessary.

Overnight Bundt Caramel Rolls

SERVES 10

●

This recipe comes from Mom's cousin Bud's daughter and has been a family favorite for years. We love to serve these rolls as part of our Christmas breakfast. Since you make them the night before, there is more time for opening presents Christmas morning!

½ cup chopped pecans

18-19 frozen, unbaked bread rolls (do not thaw)

1 package (3½ ounce) dry butterscotch pudding (not instant)

½ cup butter

¾ cup light brown sugar

¾ teaspoon cinnamon

Butter a 12-inch Bundt pan. Sprinkle bottom of pan evenly with chopped pecans. Place bread rolls in pan, making sure edges touch, filling the bottom first, then layering on top. Sprinkle pudding evenly over top of rolls. Set aside.

In a small saucepan, melt butter over low heat, then stir in the brown sugar and cinnamon. Continue cooking, stirring constantly, until sugar is dissolved. Pour butter mixture evenly over bread rolls and pudding mixture. Leave out, uncovered (do not refrigerate), overnight. (Dough will rise over the top of the pan.)

The next morning, preheat the oven to 350 degrees.

Bake the rolls for 25 to 35 minutes. Put a cookie sheet on the rack under the pan to catch any drippings. Remove from heat and let cool slightly in the pan. When ready to serve, place a serving plate over the top of the Bundt pan, and holding the plate and pan together, flip them over so the plate is on the bottom and remove the Bundt pan. The rolls hold together like a coffee cake and are topped with yummy caramel sauce and pecans. Pull the rolls apart with your hands as you serve them.

Orange Marmalade Coffee Cake

SERVES 12

A variation on the Overnight Bundt Caramel Rolls, this is every bit as delicious and easy to make. This recipe also comes from my Mom's cousin Bud's daughter.

½ cup orange marmalade
1 cup chopped pecans, separated
½ cup butter
¾ cup light brown sugar
1 teaspoon cinnamon
2 packages Pillsbury Butterflake
  dinner rolls

Preheat oven to 350 degrees. Butter a 12-inch Bundt pan.

Mix together marmalade and 1/2 cup pecans. Spread mixture on bottom of pan. Set aside.

In a small saucepan, cook butter over low heat until melted. Remove from heat. In a small bowl, stir together the brown sugar and cinnamon. Separate the rolls and dip each one first into the melted butter, then the sugar mixture and then stand on its side in the Bundt pan. Mix together the remaining butter and brown sugar mixture and pour over the top of the rolls in the pan. Sprinkle with remaining 1/2 cup nuts.

Bake for 30 minutes. Remove from heat and let cool slightly in the pan. When ready to serve, place a serving plate over the top of the bundt pan, and holding the plate and pan together, flip them over so the plate is on the bottom and remove the Bundt pan. Scrape any remaining marmalade and nuts out of the pan and spread on the top of the coffee cake.

Mixed Berry Smoothies

PER SERVING

These are delicious, easy—and good for you! If you are not a soy milk fan, you can use either regular milk or yogurt, but you will probably want to add a bit of honey as soy milk is slightly sweet. You can use any kind of berries. Also, there's no need to add ice because the berries are frozen. They, together with the banana, make the smoothies nice and thick.

½ **cup (heaping) mixed frozen**
   berries
¾ **cup soy milk**
½ **banana**

Place all ingredients in a blender and blend until well mixed. If the blender stops churning the mixture around, give it a good shake! Serve and enjoy!

A well-seasoned memory

Dad had a knack for inviting guests to impromptu dinners, and Mom always happily obliged. One time, a doctor from Japan came to study with Dad for a week. The first day he arrived, Dad invited him to dinner. Mom thought it would be wonderful to prepare a welcoming meal of spare ribs, corn on the cob and other American favorites. Upon opening the door and greeting our guest, Mom was one part happy and two parts shocked…Let's just say that the kind doctor was dentally challenged. She called for me to meet her in the kitchen where we quickly scraped the pork from the ribs to make pork sandwiches and stripped the corn off the cobs for corn pudding. Dinner saved! The next day, Mom told Dad to take his colleague to the local Japanese fish market so he could pick his favorites. He was in heaven!

Sally Clayton serving up something delicious, with Mack at her side.

soups

White Bean and Chicken Chili **page 61**

Soups are my ultimate comfort food. They are so versatile and fit the bill for any occasion. There's nothing like hot soup on a chilly winter day to warm the bones. During warmer months, a quick gazpacho is a light and refreshing way to celebrate summer's bounty. Even better, soups are the perfect dish to prepare in advance and enjoy during a busy week. All that's needed is a side salad and a crusty piece of bread. *Voilà!* Dinner is served.

Jeanne's Gazpacho

●

This recipe comes from our good friend Jeanne Saunders, who got it from her mother, who was a great cook (as is Jeanne!). It was my mom's favorite gazpacho recipe. We like to serve this refreshing soup on warm summer evenings along with a hearty salad.

2 slices white bread
4 teaspoons red wine vinegar
1 can (14 ounce) Italian-style
   tomatoes, undrained
½ green pepper, seeded, cored
   and chopped
½ medium yellow onion, peeled
   and chopped
½ teaspoon chopped garlic
¾ cup water
4 tablespoons extra virgin olive oil
4 drops Tabasco sauce
¾ teaspoon salt
½ cucumber, peeled, seeded and
   finely chopped
fresh ground pepper and paprika
   to taste

Place bread slices in a shallow pan with the vinegar and soak for 15 minutes.

Place all ingredients in a blender and mix until desired consistency. Refrigerate for at least an hour to allow flavors to blend. Season with salt and pepper as needed. Serve garnished with chopped cucumber.

MAKE AHEAD Gazpacho can be made up to 24 hours in advance, covered and refrigerated.

Gazpacho Blanco

SERVES 6

This gazpacho hits the spot for a light summer meal and pairs wonderfully with one of our main dish salads or sandwiches.

2 medium to large cucumbers,
   peeled, seeded and cut into
   1- to 2-inch pieces
½ teaspoon chopped garlic
1¼ cups chicken broth
1¼ cups sour cream
2 teaspoons rice vinegar
1 teaspoon salt
¼ cup chopped tomato, seeded
   (optional)
¼ cup chopped chives

Place the cucumber pieces and the garlic in a food processor or blender and process until puréed. Add chicken broth, sour cream, vinegar and salt. Process to blend. If using a food processor, watch carefully as the bowl will be very full and some liquid may leak out of the bottom. Season to taste with salt and pepper. Place in a container, cover and chill for at least one hour. Serve garnished with chopped tomatoes and chives.

MAKE AHEAD: Gazpacho can be made up to 2 days ahead, covered and refrigerated.

Chilled Tomato Dill Soup

SERVES 4 TO 6

This recipe is always a hit, especially on a hot summer night. I like to take it as part of a picnic dinner for a Denver Botanic Gardens summer concert, along with one of our main dish salads and a French baguette. It is rich, so small portions are best.

3 tablespoons butter

3 medium yellow onions, chopped

½ teaspoon chopped garlic

6 large ripe tomatoes, cored, seeded and quartered

¾ cups water

1½ chicken bouillon cubes

1½ tablespoons fresh dill (or 1½ teaspoon dried)

¾ cup mayonnaise

In a 2-quart saucepan, melt the butter and sauté the onion and garlic over medium heat until wilted, about 12 to 15 minutes. Add the tomatoes, water, bouillon cubes and dill, and simmer, covered, for 10 minutes. Remove from heat and cool.

Place one-half of the tomato mixture in a blender and blend until smooth. Place in a large mixing bowl. Repeat with remaining tomato mixture. Whisk in the mayonnaise and season to taste with salt and pepper. Cover and chill overnight. Serve in chilled bowls.

MAKE AHEAD Soup can be made up to two days ahead. Store covered and refrigerated.

Carrot and Zucchini Soup

SERVES 6

●

Perfect for a summer dinner affair, this soup is best served chilled. The carrots and zucchini blend beautifully and make the most of the bounty from your local farmers' market. Impress your guests at a cocktail party with a presentation of the soup passed in espresso cups.

3 medium zucchini
3 large carrots, peeled
1 cup chopped yellow onion
4 cups chicken broth
8 ounces cream cheese
½ teaspoon salt, or more to taste
¼ to ½ teaspoon ground white pepper

Slice zucchini and carrots into 1/2-inch pieces and combine with the onion and chicken broth in a large stock pot. Cover and bring to a boil. Reduce heat and simmer until vegetables are tender, about 10 minutes.

Place half of the vegetable mixture and half of the cream cheese into a blender. Blend until smooth. Place in a large bowl and repeat with remaining vegetables and cheese. Stir in salt and pepper. Bring to room temperature and then place in refrigerator to chill for at least 30 minutes before serving.

Soup can also be served hot.

MAKE AHEAD Soup can be made up to two days ahead, covered and refrigerated.

Tomato Basil Bisque

SERVES 6

●

Our local Safeway grocer sells a wonderful tomato bisque soup. We searched high and low for a recipe that duplicates it, to no avail. After several tries, we created a delicious recipe match that uses my favorite tomato bisque as a base and features butternut squash as a secret ingredient. We've also included a variation of the soup without the squash.

2 tablespoons butter
2 tablespoons extra virgin olive oil
1½ teaspoons chopped garlic
1 cup chopped yellow onion
2 cans (14.5 ounce) diced
  tomatoes with garlic and basil,
  undrained
¼ cup tomato paste
2¼ cups butternut squash
  (around 1¼ to 1½ pounds), peeled
  and diced
2 cups chicken broth
2 tablespoons chopped fresh basil
2 teaspoons fresh thyme leaves
½ teaspoon sugar
2 cups light cream
¼ teaspoon Tabasco sauce (or
  more to taste)

In a large saucepan, melt the butter with the olive oil over medium heat. Add the garlic and chopped onion and cook, stirring occasionally, until the onions are soft. Add the tomatoes, tomato paste, butternut squash, chicken broth, basil and thyme. Season to taste with the sugar, salt and pepper. Bring to a boil and then reduce heat. Cover and simmer for about 30 to 35 minutes, or until squash is fork-tender.

Purée the soup, either in the pan with an immersion blender or in a standing blender (return to the saucepan if you use the latter). Stir in 1 cup of the light cream and Tabasco; adjust seasonings as needed. Add more cream as needed to taste (Use all 2 cups for a creamier soup). Heat the soup, then ladle into bowls.

VARIATION Omit the squash, add 2 more cans of diced tomatoes, decrease the tomato paste to 2 tablespoons, decrease the chicken broth to 1 1/2 cups and increase the sugar to 1 teaspoon.

MAKE AHEAD Soup can be made up to 2 days ahead, covered and refrigerated. Reheat over medium heat.

Emergency Crab Bisque

SERVES 4

This is the ultimate in easy gourmet. The soup is put together from pantry staples. It can be difficult to find plain green pea soup without bacon or ham, so when you see it—buy it! Despite its simplicity, this soup is an impressive treat for guests.

1 can (10 ounce) Campbell's Tomato Bisque Soup, undiluted (regular tomato soup works equally well)

1 can (10 ounce) Campbell's Green Pea Soup, undiluted

1 soup can whole milk

½ soup can light cream

¼ cup dry sherry

8 ounces lump crabmeat (cooked lobster meat or chopped cooked chicken or sausage can be substituted for the crab)

In a large saucepan over medium heat, whisk together the two soups. Whisk in milk, cream and then sherry. Combine thoroughly. Stir in crabmeat. Add salt and pepper to taste. Heat thoroughly but do not boil.

A well-seasoned memory

Mom and Dad loved international travel. They typically had friends in the countries they visited which allowed them to gain a good understanding of the local culture and politics. For Mom, that meant getting to know the local cuisine. After returning home, they would host a dinner party at which mom would serve a local dish from the country they visited, and Dad would narrate a slide show of their pictures and talk about what they had learned. It was always interesting, delicious and quite entertaining for all.

Mom overseeing the final preparations for a dinner party in Egypt.

Indian Mulligatawny Soup

This is my modification of an old recipe of Mom's. My update of the traditional favorite includes carrot and celery. *(Cover photo)*

8 tablespoons butter

1 cup finely chopped yellow onion

4 celery ribs, finely chopped

2 large carrots, peeled and finely chopped

3 tablespoons flour

4 teaspoons curry powder

8 cups chicken broth

¾ cup white or brown rice

1 apple, cored and finely chopped

2 skinless, boneless chicken breast halves, cut into ¼-inch pieces

¼ teaspoon fresh thyme

1 cup half and half

In a large stock pot, melt the butter. Add the chopped onion, celery and carrots and sauté over medium to medium-high heat until the onions are softened, around 10 minutes. Stir in the flour and curry powder and continue cooking, stirring occasionally, for an additional 5 minutes. Stir in the chicken broth and bring to a boil. Reduce heat and simmer for 30 minutes.

Add the rice, apple, chicken, thyme and salt and pepper to taste (you won't need much salt). Bring to a boil again, reduce heat and simmer for 15 minutes. Stir in the cream, bring to a boil again, reduce and simmer for another 5 to 10 minutes or until the rice is done. Let cool for a few minutes before serving—it gets very hot!

MAKE AHEAD Soup can be made up to 24 hours in advance, cooled to room temperature, covered and refrigerated. Reheat over medium heat.

Corn and Chicken Chowder

SERVES 6

●

A wonderful variation of a traditional chicken chowder recipe. Serve with Nama's Rolls on the side.

2 slices bacon
1 pound skinned, boned chicken breasts, cut into ½-inch pieces
1 cup chopped red bell pepper
1 cup chopped yellow onion
1 teaspoon chopped garlic
4½ cups chicken broth
1¾ cups peeled, diced red potatoes
2¼ cups frozen whole-kernel corn
2 cups milk (can use regular or low-fat)
½ cup flour
1 cup sharp Cheddar cheese

Fry bacon in the bottom of a large stockpot over medium heat until crisp. Remove from pot and drain on paper towel; crumble and set aside. Don't clean out pot.

Add the chicken, bell pepper, onion and garlic to the stockpot and cook in the bacon fat over medium heat for 5 minutes. Add the broth and potatoes, and bring to a boil. Cover, reduce heat and simmer 20 minutes or until the potatoes are tender. Stir in the corn.

Place milk in a medium mixing bowl and slowly sift the flour into the milk, whisking it in as you go. Slowly stir milk mixture into soup. Cook over medium heat until thick, around 15 minutes, stirring often. Stir in cheese; add salt and pepper to taste. Ladle into individual bowls and top with crumbled bacon.

MAKE AHEAD Chowder can be made earlier in the day and reheated prior to serving.

White Bean and Chicken Chili

SERVES 6 TO 8

Traditional chili dishes can often take several hours to make. This lighter version takes no time at all and uses chicken and white beans instead of ground beef and kidney beans. Warmed flour tortillas make a nice accompaniment. *(Photo, page 50)*

CHILI
3 pounds boneless, skinless
   chicken thighs
1½ teaspoons white pepper
1 teaspoon garlic powder
3 tablespoons vegetable oil
1 small yellow onion, diced
2 cans (15 ounce) Great Northern
   beans
2 cans (14½ ounce) chicken broth
2 cans (4½ ounce) chopped green
   chilies
1 can (10¾ ounce) cream of
   chicken soup
3 tablespoons jalapeño pepper
   juice (from a jar of pickled
   jalapeño peppers)
2 tablespoons chopped
   fresh cilantro
1 teaspoon salt

GARNISH
1 cup sour cream
1½ cups grated mozzarella cheese
   (about 6 ounces)
½ cup minced fresh cilantro
Slices of pickled jalapeño peppers
   (optional)

Cut chicken into small pieces and season with white pepper and garlic powder. Sauté chicken in oil in a stockpot for three minutes. Add remaining chili ingredients through the salt and bring to a boil. Reduce heat and simmer for 30 minutes.

To serve, ladle chili into bowls and garnish with sour cream, cheese, cilantro and a slice of jalapeño pepper (if desired).

MAKE AHEAD Chili can be made up to 24 hours in advance, cooled to room temperature, covered and refrigerated. Reheat over medium heat.

salads

Roasted Tomato and Arugula Salad page 71

Growing up, every dinner in our home included a salad—Dad insisted on it! As a result, our recipe file is packed full of interesting ways to prepare them. Like all side dishes, the salad should complement other foods being served, especially the main dish. Because of this, some of our salads are simple. Some feature meat and others, fruit, providing the ultimate flexibility in planning a menu. Just as scrumptious, we love main-dish salads, especially for picnic dinners, luncheons and light summer fare. We're also fans of layered salads, as they're so delicious and great time-savers with their advanced preparation.

Spinach and Goat Cheese Salad

SERVES 6

The mustard greens in this recipe give this spinach salad a different flavor than the norm. We love the combination of the greens, spinach, goat cheese and cranberries.

DRESSING

3 tablespoons olive oil
2 tablespoons honey
¼ cup fresh lemon juice
½ teaspoon minced garlic
½ teaspoon salt
¼ teaspoon fresh ground pepper

SALAD

3 cups torn spinach leaves
1 cup torn mustard greens
2 cups torn red leaf lettuce
½ to ¾ cup sliced red onion
6 tablespoons goat cheese
    crumbles
6 tablespoons dried cranberries

Combine olive oil, honey, lemon juice, garlic, salt and pepper in a small jar with a lid. Whisk until well combined. Cover and set aside.

In a large salad bowl, toss the spinach, mustard greens and red leaf lettuce. Toss with the dressing. Arrange tossed salad on 6 salad plates, top with onion rings, goat cheese (1 tablespoon per serving) and dried cranberries (1 tablespoon per serving). Season with salt and pepper.

MAKE AHEAD Dressing can be made several days ahead, stored in the jar and refrigerated. Bring to room temperature before using.

Spinach Salad with Lemon-Dijon Dressing

SERVES 6

●

This recipe comes from Gary Hardin, an excellent cook and even better friend I knew when living in Amsterdam.

2 hard boiled eggs
handful of fresh green herbs—
   combination of parsley, chives,
   tarragon and chervil
2 tablespoons lemon zest
¼ teaspoon salt (or more to taste)
½ tablespoon Dijon mustard
1 tablespoon freshly squeezed
   lemon juice (or more to taste)
½ cup extra virgin olive oil
4 to 6 cups fresh baby spinach

Finely dice the eggs and herbs; mix together in a bowl and season to taste with salt and pepper. Set aside.

In a small bowl, mash together the lemon zest and salt (works best with a mortar and pestle but use a fork if you don't have one). Whisk in the mustard and the lemon juice. Slowly whisk in the oil. Add additional salt, lemon juice and fresh ground pepper to taste. Toss the spinach with the dressing. Divide among 6 individual salad plates and sprinkle egg and herb mixture over the top.

VARIATION Can substitute any salad greens for the spinach.

MAKE AHEAD Dressing can be made up to 24 hours ahead, covered and refrigerated.

Avocado and Grapefruit Salad

SERVES 8 TO 10

This was one of Mom's favorite salads to serve as a first course because it is so pretty. It's also very refreshing on a hot summer day. If you want to serve it as a side dish or on a buffet, simply coarsely chop the grapefruit and avocado and toss the salad instead of arranging it.

DRESSING
½ cup extra virgin olive oil
¼ cup red wine vinegar
¼ cup sugar
½ teaspoon salt
½ teaspoon celery seed
½ teaspoon dry mustard

SALAD
2 ripe avocadoes
1 head green leaf lettuce
1 head red leaf lettuce
2 cups fresh pink grapefruit
   sections (or a mixture of
   pink, white and red)
½ cup chopped red onion

Combine olive oil, vinegar, sugar, salt, celery seed and dry mustard in a medium sized jar and whisk until well blended. Cover and set aside.

Peel and slice the avocadoes. Wash, dry and tear the lettuces into bite-sized pieces and place in a large bowl. Toss with part of the dressing. Divide among 8 to 10 individual salad plates. Top with avocado slices and grapefruit sections, forming a pinwheel pattern. Sprinkle the chopped onion on the top. Drizzle with remaining dressing and serve.

MAKE AHEAD Dressing can be made several days ahead and refrigerated. Bring to room temperature before using.

Hearts of Romaine with Lemon-Anchovy Dressing

SERVES 8

●

A wonderfully light side salad that pairs well with a rich entrée. Croutons or toasted pine nuts will provide additional flavor, but it is delicious just as is!

¼ cup extra virgin olive oil

2 tablespoons fresh lemon juice

1 teaspoon Lea & Perrins Marinade for Chicken*

1 teaspoon Dijon mustard

½ teaspoon chopped garlic

1 teaspoon anchovy paste or 1 anchovy, rinsed, drained and mashed

3 to 4 romaine hearts

¼ cup Parmesan cheese, or more to taste

This sauce was originally called "White Wine Worcestershire Sauce" and is available in specialty food stores. If you can't find it, use regular Worcestershire sauce.

In a jar with a fitted lid, whisk together the olive oil, lemon juice, Marinade, mustard, garlic and anchovy paste. Cover and store in the refrigerator.

When ready to serve, tear the romaine hearts into bite-sized pieces and place in a large salad bowl. Toss with the Parmesan cheese and enough dressing to coat. Season to taste with salt, pepper and more cheese as needed.

MAKE AHEAD Dressing can be made several days ahead, covered and stored in the refrigerator. Bring to room temperature before using.

Red Leaf Lettuce with Hot Bacon Dressing

SERVES 4

•

Mom had been making this salad since I was a little girl, and my brother and I still frequently make it—it is timeless and always receives rave reviews. This is a classic Sally Clayton meal when paired with flank steak prepared with Mom's Steak and Lamb Marinade, Kentucky Corn Pudding and Nama's Rolls.

4 slices bacon
2 tablespoons chopped fresh
 parsley
5 tablespoons red wine or
 cider vinegar
1 tablespoon chopped chives
1 tablespoon chopped green onion
1 tablespoon sugar
2 tablespoons water
1 head red leaf lettuce, torn

Fry bacon in a small skillet until crisp. Remove cooked bacon from pan, reserving drippings in pan; crumble bacon when cool.

Let bacon drippings cool slightly. Whisk in parsley, vinegar, chives, green onion, sugar, water, and salt and pepper to taste. When ready to serve, bring mixture to a boil and pour over lettuce. Sprinkle with crumbled bacon.

A well-seasoned memory

•

Red, ripe, juicy strawberries were one of Mom's favorites. One year, she decided to grow her own. Early in the summer, slugs began to eat the crop she had so carefully tended. A friend advised that the best way to control the slugs was to bury an empty coffee can full of beer next to the plants. The idea was that the slugs would be attracted to the beer, fall in the can and drown. Well, despite Mom's best efforts, the slugs still ate the berries. In her typical fashion, she shrugged it off by saying that at least the slugs died happy—full of her favorite fruit and buzzed on beer!

Sally at home in her Colorado kitchen.

Cilantro Peanut Coleslaw

SERVES 8

●

A refreshing and healthy summer salad. Add grilled chicken or shrimp to turn this into a main dish.

1 cup peanut oil

1¼ cups roasted peanuts, divided

Juice from 1 lemon (or more to taste, and depending on size of lemon)

¼ cup rice wine vinegar

1 teaspoon minced fresh ginger

2 tablespoons sugar

6 green onions, divided

1 cup fresh cilantro leaves, divided (packed or not, to taste)

1 teaspoon salt

4 cups shredded green cabbage

4 cups shredded purple cabbage

1 small jicama, peeled and sliced into ⅛-inch strips

Make the dressing first. Put the peanut oil, 1/2 cup of the roasted peanuts, lemon juice, rice vinegar, ginger, sugar, 2 green onions coarsely chopped, 1/2 cup cilantro and salt into a food processor and process until thoroughly mixed and the peanuts are ground up. Place in a covered container in the refrigerator for at least one hour before serving.

In a large salad bowl, toss together the shredded cabbage and jicama. Chop the remaining 4 green onions coarsely and add to the salad along with the remaining 1/2 cup cilantro and remaining 3/4 cup roasted peanuts. Just before serving, toss salad with the dressing. Add salt and pepper as needed.

MAKE AHEAD Dressing can be made up to 1 day ahead, covered and refrigerated.

Roasted Tomato and Arugula Salad

SERVES 6 TO 8

A wonderfully refreshing salad that looks beautiful. This recipe comes from our friend Liane Clasen who loves it for its versatility. Add roasted pine nuts or bacon bits if you like. *(Photo, page 62)*

8 plum tomatoes
1 teaspoon chopped rosemary
1 teaspoon fresh thyme, chopped
1½ teaspoons kosher salt, divided
¼ cup + 4 teaspoons extra virgin olive oil, divided
2 tablespoons balsamic vinegar
½ teaspoon chopped garlic
8 cups baby arugula leaves
8 ounces fresh buffalo mozzarella
½ cup pitted Kalamata (or other type) black olives, cut in half if large

Preheat oven to 400 degrees. Line a rimmed baking sheet with parchment paper.

Cut tomatoes in half crosswise. Trim bottoms so they can sit upright. Gently squeeze out seeds. Place tomatoes, cut side up, on prepared baking sheet. Sprinkle with rosemary, thyme and 1 teaspoon of the salt. Drizzle 4 teaspoons of olive oil over the tomatoes. Roast for 45 minutes. Set aside to cool.

While the tomatoes are roasting, prepare the dressing: in a jar with a fitted lid, blend together the balsamic vinegar, garlic, remaining 1/2 teaspoon salt and 1/4 cup olive oil. Add fresh ground pepper to taste. Cover and store in the refrigerator. Bring to room temperature before using.

When ready to serve the salad, toss some of the dressing with the arugula and arrange on a large serving platter. Top with roasted tomatoes, roasted side up. Gently cut cheese into slices (and then cut in half if large) and arrange around the tomatoes on the arugula. Sprinkle with olives and drizzle with more dressing. Season with more salt and pepper as needed.

MAKE AHEAD Tomatoes can be roasted earlier in the day and kept at room temperature until serving. Balsamic dressing can be made several days ahead and stored in a closed jar in the refrigerator.

Tomatoes Stuffed with Artichoke Hearts, Onions and Bacon

SERVES 6

●

A wonderful side dish on a warm summer night. Great for a buffet or for taking along to a potluck.

2 cups canned water-packed
   artichoke hearts, drained and
   coarsely chopped
1 cup mayonnaise
½ cup finely chopped celery
½ cup chopped green onion
¼ cup grated Parmesan cheese
6 to 8 medium tomatoes
3 slices bacon, cooked and
   crumbled

In a medium mixing bowl, stir together the artichoke hearts, mayonnaise, celery, onion and cheese. Season with salt and pepper to taste. Cover and refrigerate until ready to use.

Cut the top off the tomatoes and scoop out the insides (a grapefruit spoon works well), making sure not to cut through the sides or the bottom. Turn upside down and place on paper towel to drain for at least 30 minutes. Sprinkle the insides with salt and pepper. Stuff with artichoke mixture. Sprinkle crumbled bacon on top.

MAKE AHEAD The artichoke mixture can be prepared up to one day in advance and stored, covered, in the refrigerator. You can also stuff the tomatoes earlier in the day you are serving them and store, covered, in the refrigerator.

Broccoli Salad with Caesar Dressing

SERVES 8

This summer salad is perfect for a picnic or buffet. It also is a refreshing option for a potluck dinner.

SALAD

6 cups fresh broccoli florets
   (about 3 large bunches)
½ cup sliced black olives
   (2 ¼-ounce cans)
1 medium red onion, thinly sliced
1 medium red bell pepper, seeded
   and thinly sliced

DRESSING

2 teaspoons Dijon mustard
2 egg yolks
2 teaspoons chopped garlic
1 teaspoon capers
6 tablespoons freshly grated
   Parmesan cheese
2 sprigs parsley
3 anchovy fillets, drained
1 cup extra virgin olive oil
2 tablespoons fresh lemon juice
¼ cup red wine vinegar

Steam the broccoli until crisp-tender, 3 to 4 minutes. Plunge immediately into a bowl of ice water. Drain, place in a large serving bowl and toss with olives, onion and pepper.

To make the dressing, place the mustard, egg yolks, garlic, capers, Parmesan, parsley and anchovies in a food processor and blend until well mixed. With the machine running slowly add the lemon juice and vinegar, then add the olive oil. Season to taste with salt and pepper (shouldn't need much salt). Pour over the broccoli mixture and toss. Chill for at least 2 hours before serving.

MAKE AHEAD The dressing can be made up to one day ahead, covered and refrigerated. Bring to room temperature before using.

Curried Pea Salad

SERVES 4 TO 6

●

A modern version of a classic dish, you'll find this to be a very satisfying summer salad. It pairs wonderfully with grilled chicken, but it complements just about any main dish. If you prefer, substitute turkey bacon for the regular. Consider adding a bit of salt if you use unsalted cashews.

1 package (10 ounce) frozen baby peas (about 2 cups)

5 tablespoons chopped green onions (around 4 or 5)

½ cup chopped celery

3 slices bacon, cooked and crumbled

⅔ cup sour cream

1½ teaspoons curry powder (or more, depending on the strength of your curry powder)

½ to ¾ teaspoon salt

½ teaspoon ground pepper

½ cup salted roasted cashews, coarsely chopped

Place the peas in a colander under hot running water until thawed and not crunchy; drain, dry and discard any peas that look dried out. In a medium mixing bowl, stir together the peas, onions, celery and bacon.

In a small mixing bowl, whisk together the sour cream, curry powder, salt and pepper. Stir into the pea mixture just until coated. Gently stir in the cashews and adjust the curry powder and salt to taste just before serving. Can be served cold or at room temperature.

MAKE AHEAD Salad can be made earlier in the day and stored, covered, in the refrigerator.

Minted Green Beans with Feta and Pecans

SERVES 8 TO 10

●

This dish is best made when fresh mint is in season, adding lots of flavor. For a short cut, I like to use prepared green beans that come in a bag (in the produce section of most markets). Just follow the directions on the bag for microwaving the beans instead of steaming them.

DRESSING
¾ cup olive oil
½ cup fresh mint leaves (packed)
¼ cup white wine vinegar
¾ teaspoon salt
½ teaspoon minced garlic
¼ teaspoon black pepper

SALAD
1½ pounds fresh green beans,
  cleaned, cut into 1-inch pieces
1 cup chopped, toasted pecans
  (can substitute walnuts)
1 cup chopped red onion
1 cup crumbled feta cheese
  (not flavored)

Combine the olive oil, mint, vinegar, salt, garlic and pepper in a food processor or blender and blend until smooth. Add salt and pepper to taste. Put in a jar or other covered container and chill.

Steam the green beans until crisp-tender. Drain and plunge them into ice water to keep their bright green color. Drain again and pat dry with paper towel; cool. When cooled and dried, place in a serving bowl and toss with the pecans, onion and cheese. Cover and chill for at least one hour (or longer).

Just before serving, pour the mint dressing over the salad and toss. Season with salt and pepper.

MAKE AHEAD The dressing can be made up to 3 days ahead, kept covered in the refrigerator. The beans can be cooked one day ahead and kept in a ziploc baggie in the refrigerator. Toss with the pecans, onions and cheese the day you plan to serve.

Sharp Vinaigrette Dressing

MAKES ABOUT 3/4 CUP

Growing up with Mom's homemade salad dressings, it's hard for me to use purchased. We always have this dressing on hand and use it nearly every day. It's very refreshing with just the right amount of "bite" to it. For a different, slightly sweeter flavor, you can substitute balsamic vinegar for the white wine vinegar.

½ cup extra virgin olive oil
¼ cup white wine vinegar or
    tarragon vinegar
2 tablespoons Dijon mustard
¼ teaspoon salt
1 to 1½ teaspoons chopped garlic

Place all ingredients in a medium jar with a fitted lid. Blend until well combined. Store covered in the refrigerator. Bring to room temperature before serving.

MAKE AHEAD Dressing will keep, covered, in the refrigerator for several weeks.

Grilled Chicken and Green Bean Salad

(SERVES 8 TO 10)

●

This is a refreshing salad that is easy to make, is good for you, and doesn't take much time. You can have this one-dish dinner on the table in less than an hour. It's yummy served with Jeanne's Gazpacho as the first course and any kind of bread on the side. And, it's portable. One year, I served this menu on a party boat on Steamboat Lake for Mom's birthday.

SALAD
¼ cup + 1 tablespoon extra virgin olive oil, divided
¼ cup + 1 tablespoon soy sauce, divided
8 boneless, skinless chicken breast halves
2 microwaveable bags (12 ounce) trimmed green beans*
1 cup red grape tomatoes, sliced in half
½ cup chopped red onion
1½ cups chopped roasted pecans

DRESSING
1½ tablespoons Dijon mustard
1½ tablespoons balsamic vinegar
½ cup extra virgin olive oil

TOPPING
2 tablespoons chopped fresh thyme
6 to 8 ounces fresh goat cheese crumbles

Available in most markets in the produce section. If not, cook 1½ pounds regular green beans in boiling salt water for 5 to 7 minutes, or until crisp-tender.

Preheat grill.

Mix together 1/4 cup olive oil and 1/4 cup soy sauce. If chicken breasts are very thick at one end, pound to more of an even thickness. Brush soy-oil mixture on both sides of chicken breasts and season both sides with salt and pepper. Grill chicken breasts over medium heat for 5 minutes, flip and cook until done, about another 5 to 6 minutes. Place chicken on a cutting board and cut into bite-size pieces. Mix together remaining 1 tablespoon of soy sauce and 1 tablespoon of olive oil and brush over cut pieces. Set aside.

While the chicken is on the grill, microwave green beans according to package instructions until crisp-tender. Place cooked beans in a colander and rinse under cold water. Drain, pat dry with paper towels and cut into 1-inch pieces. Place in a large mixing bowl and add the chicken, tomatoes, red onion, and chopped pecans. Toss to combine (works best if done with your hands).

To make the dressing, whisk together in a small bowl the mustard, vinegar and 1/2 cup olive oil. Sprinkle the chicken and green beans with the thyme. Add the dressing and toss. Season to taste with salt and pepper. Place on serving dish (or individual plates), sprinkle the top with goat cheese and serve. This salad tastes best if you let it sit at room temperature for about an hour before serving, but this isn't required.

MAKE AHEAD Grill the chicken, cook green beans, and make the dressing up to one day ahead. Store separately in the refrigerator and mix together the day you are serving.

Layered Chicken Salad with Tarragon Dressing

SERVES 8

●

This classic recipe of Mom's is a great make-ahead dish for a luncheon or casual summer dinner. Serve it with fresh rolls or croissants. Try to use fresh tarragon and basil rather than substituting dried herbs for this recipe—it will taste much better. Note that this dish needs to be made several hours ahead, and can be made the day before.

TARRAGON DRESSING

1½ cups mayonnaise
1½ tablespoons Dijon mustard
2½ teaspoons chopped fresh
   tarragon
1½ teaspoons chopped fresh basil
¼ teaspoon ground pepper

CHICKEN SALAD

1 medium head napa cabbage,
   chopped (see Note)
8 ounces sliced mushrooms
2½ cups shredded, cooked
   chicken*
⅓ cup chopped red onion
1 package (10 ounce) frozen peas,
   thawed & drained
1 medium cucumber, peeled
   and chopped
1 pint cherry tomatoes, cut in half

About the same amount as from one purchased rotisserie chicken.

For the dressing, in a large medium bowl, whisk together the mayonnaise, mustard, tarragon, basil and pepper. Season to taste with salt and more pepper (may not need any salt). Set aside.

Spread the chopped cabbage in the bottom of a shallow, 3-quart casserole or serving dish (a pretty 9x12-inch dish works well). Sprinkle lightly with salt. Top with the mushrooms, then chicken, then onion, then peas and scatter cucumber over the top. Again, sprinkle lightly with salt. Spread dressing evenly over the top. Garnish with cherry tomato halves, cut side up (you may not need the entire pint—it depends on the size of the tomatoes). Cover and chill at least 4 hours or overnight.

NOTE Napa cabbage is oval-shaped and lighter in color than regular cabbage, and the leaves are wrinkly and slightly curled on the edges.

Overnight Chicken Taco Salad

(SERVES 8 TO 10)

Mom was a huge fan of overnight salads, as am I. They not only save on time, the flavors blend well overnight. This salad works equally well for family meals and entertaining. Add purchased salsa, either on top of the dressing or on the side, if you want to spice it up a bit.

CHICKEN TACO SALAD

4 cups shredded lettuce

2 cups chopped cooked chicken (see Note)

2 cups chopped fresh tomato

1 cup sliced ripe olives

2 green onions, chopped

2 cups shredded cheese, mixture of Cheddar and Monterey jack

Crushed tortilla chips

AVOCADO DRESSING

2 avocadoes, peeled and pitted

¾ cup plain yogurt

3 tablespoons freshly squeezed lime juice

1 garlic clove, minced

1½ teaspoon chili powder

½ teaspoon salt

½ teaspoon ground cumin

Dash Tabasco sauce

In a deep 3- or 4-quart glass bowl, layer lettuce, chicken, tomato, olives and onions. Sprinkle with salt and pepper. Set aside.

In a food processor, purée avocadoes until smooth. Add yogurt, lime juice, garlic, chili powder, salt, cumin and Tabasco sauce; blend just two or three turns to mix. Add salt and pepper as needed. Spread over top of onions. Sprinkle cheese on top. Cover and chill for several hours or overnight. Sprinkle with crushed tortilla chips just before serving. If desired, you can toss the salad before serving.

NOTE This is especially good if you cook the chicken with taco seasoning. Chop 2 to 3 chicken breast halves (amount depends on their size) and cook over medium heat in a mixture of vegetable oil and taco seasoning.

Layered Chinese Chicken Salad

SERVES 10 TO 12

●

Preparing this salad the night before you plan to serve it makes a busy day a little easier. Mom loved to serve this recipe at luncheons. It was a favorite when she played bridge—she didn't have to stop playing to cook lunch!

SALAD

6 cups shredded lettuce (iceberg, butter and/or romaine)

¼ pound bean sprouts

1 can (8 ounce) sliced water chestnuts, drained and coarsely chopped

½ cup sliced green onion

1 medium cucumber, thinly sliced and quartered

4 cups cooked chicken, shredded or cubed

2 packages (6 ounce) frozen Chinese pea pods, thawed

DRESSING

2 cups mayonnaise

2 teaspoons curry powder (or more, depending on the strength of your curry powder)

1 tablespoon sugar

½ teaspoon ground ginger

GARNISH

½ cup Spanish-style peanuts, chopped

18 small cherry or grape tomatoes, halved

In a shallow, 4-quart serving dish (preferably glass because the salad is pretty!), spread shredded lettuce in an even layer. Sprinkle with salt and pepper. Top with bean sprouts, then water chestnuts, then green onion, then cucumber, and chicken last. Dry pea pods, cut in half and arrange on top. Sprinkle with salt and pepper.

In a small bowl, whisk together mayonnaise, curry powder, sugar and ginger. Season to taste with salt and pepper. Spread mixture evenly over pea pods. Cover and refrigerate for 24 hours. Garnish top with peanuts and tomatoes before serving.

Chilled Asian Chicken and Noodles

●

I love this salad for casual summer dinner parties as it's so easy to make ahead. It also easily doubles for a large crowd.

SALAD
1 pound linguine or spaghetti
¼ cup dark sesame oil
8 cooked chicken breast halves, chopped
2 bunches green onions
1 bunch fresh cilantro
2 jalapeño peppers
⅜ pound fresh snow peas, thinly sliced length-wise

DRESSING
½ cup soy sauce
¼ cup creamy peanut butter (not fresh ground or old fashioned)
¼ cup rice vinegar
¼ cup dark sesame oil
1 tablespoon sugar

Cook pasta in boiling salted water until *al dente*. Drain, rinse well and transfer to large mixing bowl. Stir in 1/4 cup sesame oil, toss well, and then add cooked chicken. Slice green onions, chop cilantro and add both to pasta mixture. Seed, devein and mince jalapeño and add to pasta mixture. Set aside.

Cook snow peas in boiling salted water for about one minute, until crisp-tender. Drain, rinse well and toss into salad.

For dressing, combine soy sauce, peanut butter, vinegar, sesame oil and sugar in blender or food processor and blend until smooth. Pour dressing over salad and toss well. Season to taste with salt and pepper.

NOTE Can easily be doubled to serve 20 people.

MAKE AHEAD Pasta salad an be made one day ahead, covered and refrigerated.

Avocado and Crab Salad

SERVES 4

●

We love this recipe, especially on a warm summer night when we don't want to turn on the oven or heat the stove top! For a more formal presentation, Mom recommended placing a peeled and pitted avocado half on mixed salad greens on each plate, and topping with a mound of crab salad.

DRESSING
½ cup mayonnaise
½ cup sour cream
¾ teaspoon curry powder
   (or more, depending on how
   strong your curry powder is)

SALAD
1 pound fresh Dungeness crabmeat
¼ cup green onions, sliced
1 can (8 ounce) sliced water
   chestnuts, chopped
6 to 8 dashes Tabasco sauce
½ cup pine nuts, lightly toasted
2 ripe avocados
4 cups mixed salad greens

Make the dressing by blending the mayonnaise, sour cream and curry powder in a food processor or blender. Add salt and pepper to taste. Refrigerate for 30 minutes to allow the flavors to set.

Stir together the crabmeat with enough dressing to make the mixture creamy. Stir in green onions, water chestnuts, Tabasco and pine nuts. Peel, pit and coarsely chop the avocadoes and carefully fold into the crabmeat mixture. Add salt and pepper as needed.

Divide salad greens among 4 serving plates. Place the avocado and crab mixture on top and serve immediately. Alternatively, you can put the greens on a serving plate with the crab on top. Pass extra dressing, if any remains, on the side.

Rice, Shrimp and Avocado Salad

SERVES 6

●

A delicious cold curry dish, complete with crunchy apple and cashews. Mom loved to put this in pita rounds and take it for tailgating before a Denver Broncos game. You can easily expand this dish to serve 8 or even 10—just add another 1/2 pound. shrimp, 1/4 cup rice and 1/2 apple. Note directions below for what to do with the leftover mayonnaise sauce.

SALAD

1½ pounds small to medium shrimp, cooked

1¾ cups cooked long grain white rice (can also use brown rice)

1½ large green apples, cored and finely chopped

1 avocado, peeled and chopped

½ cup salted cashews, chopped

⅓ cup chopped green onion

DRESSING

1 cup mayonnaise

⅔ cup sour cream

2 teaspoons curry powder (or more, depending on how strong your curry powder is)

Chop the cooked shrimp if it is not bite-sized. In a large mixing bowl, combine shrimp with the rice, apple, avocado, cashews and green onion.

In a small mixing bowl, whisk together the mayonnaise, sour cream and curry powder. Stir just 1/2 the curry sauce into the shrimp mixture and fold until well mixed. Stir in remaining sauce only if needed. (You probably won't need the other half.) Season to taste with salt and pepper. Chill for at least 3 hours.

Line a serving platter with lettuce leaves. Mound salad on top. For a prettier presentation, place large lettuce leaves on small luncheon plates and mound individual portions of salad on top.

VARIATION This salad is delicious stuffed inside pita rounds. Cut off one end of each of 6 pitas and stuff with the salad.

MAKE AHEAD The salad can be made earlier in the day and stored, covered, in the refrigerator.

NOTE You will likely have leftover curry-mayonnaise sauce from this recipe. Save it, then spread it on a fresh fish filet (like halibut or swordfish) and grill the fish over medium heat. Sprinkle with chopped fresh herbs (whatever you have on hand—chives, tarragon, parsley, dill, etc.). Two dishes from one recipe!

Smoked Fish and Pasta Salad

SERVES 4

●

A wonderful fresh, unusual summer salad. I like to lightly toss the arugula with olive oil before topping it with the pasta salad.

¼ pound dry pasta (corkscrew or shells)
2 tablespoons extra virgin olive oil
½ cup buttermilk
½ cup mayonnaise
3 tablespoons prepared horseradish
¼ cup chopped fresh dill
1½ cups seeded and chopped plum tomatoes
2 tablespoons capers, drained and rinsed
1 cup chopped red onion
12 ounces smoked fish (we like trout), skinned, boned and cut into ½-inch pieces
Lemon juice (optional)
Arugula

Cook the pasta according to the package directions until *al dente* (done but still slightly firm). Drain, rinse with cold water, drain again. Transfer to a large mixing bowl and toss with the olive oil.

In a separate large bowl, whisk together the buttermilk, mayonnaise, horseradish and dill. Add the pasta, tomatoes, capers and red onion and toss. Carefully fold in the trout. Season to taste with salt, pepper and lemon juice if desired. Serve on a bed of arugula.

MAKE AHEAD Pasta salad can be made earlier in the day, covered and refrigerated. Bring to room temperature before placing on the arugula.

poultry

Chicken is a staple in our household for both weeknights and weekend gatherings. It's versatile, easy to prepare and nutritious. The challenge is finding new ways to prepare it! The good news is that, with a little inspiration, choices are endless. You can beat chicken boredom by adding a few fresh recipes to your repertoire. I've included our family favorites here to inspire you, whether you're saucing, stuffing or skewering your chicken for your next meal.

Grilled Chicken with Tomatoes and Goat Cheese

SERVES 4

●

This serves as an excellent, refreshing dish on a hot summer evening, especially toward the end of the summer when fresh tomatoes are plentiful. *(Photo, page 88)*

1 cup yellow grape or cherry tomatoes, halved

1 cup red grape or cherry tomatoes, halved

¼ teaspoon sea salt

2 ounces mild goat cheese (flavored works well), crumbled, divided

3 tablespoons extra virgin olive oil, divided

4 boneless, skinless chicken breast halves, pounded if thick

Preheat a grill or broiler.

Put the tomatoes in a colander set over a medium mixing bowl. Toss with the sea salt and let stand for at least 20 minutes to release the juices. Remove and set aside the colander; into the collected juice from the tomatoes, whisk half the goat cheese and 2 tablespoons of the olive oil until smooth. Fold in the tomatoes and remaining goat cheese. Season with freshly ground pepper.

Brush the chicken breasts with the remaining 1 tablespoon of olive oil and season with salt and pepper. Grill or broil on high heat for 5 minutes per side, or until cooked through. Serve with the tomato-goat cheese mixture on top.

Grilled Chicken with Lime-Green Chile Sauce

SERVES 4

●

Our friend Tamara O'Brien recommends serving this dish with fresh corn tortillas on the side to mop up the extra sauce. Adding refried beans, rice and a tossed green salad will round out an easy weeknight meal.

¼ cup Dijon mustard
¼ cup olive oil, divided
2 tablespoons chopped fresh Italian parsley
4 boneless, skinless chicken breast halves
1¼ cups chopped green onions (around one bunch)
1 shallot, chopped
½ teaspoon chopped garlic
1 whole roasted green chile (okay to use canned)
1 cup chopped fresh cilantro
1 cup chicken broth
4 teaspoons fresh lime juice

In a small bowl, whisk together the mustard, 3 tablespoons of the olive oil and the parsley.

Pound the chicken breasts between two sheets of waxed paper to an even thickness (but not too thin). Generously brush mustard mixture on both sides of the chicken breasts. Set breasts in a glass baking dish, cover with plastic wrap and refrigerate for at least 30 minutes.

In a medium skillet, heat remaining 1 tablespoon olive oil and cook the chopped green onions, shallot and garlic over medium-low heat, stirring occasionally, for 4 minutes. Put the onion mixture, green chili, cilantro and chicken broth in a blender and purée until smooth. Return the mixture to the skillet you cooked the onions in, stir in lime juice and season with salt and pepper to taste. Warm sauce over low heat while you are cooking the chicken—it will cook down a bit and concentrate the flavors.

Grill chicken breasts over medium heat, or broil them, for around 4 to 6 minutes per side (depending on thickness of breasts) until cooked through. Slice and serve on top of sauce.

MAKE AHEAD Sauce can be made up to 24 hours ahead, covered and refrigerated. Reheat over medium heat.

Chicken with Mushrooms, Scallions and Almonds

SERVES 4

●

Mushrooms, wine and cream make an especially flavorful sauce for this rich chicken dish. Wonderful in autumn accompanied by roasted potatoes.

4 skinless, boneless chicken
   breast halves
½ teaspoon fresh ground pepper
1 teaspoon garlic-flavored (or
   regular) olive oil
1 cup dry white wine
4 cups sliced fresh mushrooms
¼ cup sour cream
¼ cup sliced green onions
4 tablespoons toasted slivered
   almonds

Place chicken breasts between sheets of wax paper and, with a meat mallet or rolling pin, pound chicken slightly to a more uniform thickness. Season on both sides with ground pepper. In a large nonstick skillet, heat the oil over high heat and sauté the chicken breasts, turning once, until browned, about 1 minute per side. Add the wine to the chicken in the skillet, reduce the heat to low, cover and simmer until the chicken is just cooked throughout but still moist, about 7 to 8 minutes. Remove the chicken from the pan and keep warm. Pour the cooking liquid into a cup and reserve.

Add the mushrooms to the skillet and cook over high heat, without stirring, until browned on the bottom, about 1 1/2 minutes. Add the reserved cooking liquid and boil until almost all the liquid is gone, about 2 to 3 minutes. Add any juices that have drained from the chicken. Remove from the heat and stir in sour cream and green onions. Season to taste with salt and pepper. Pour mushroom mixture over chicken, garnish with toasted almonds and serve.

Chicken Breasts Stuffed with Chorizo
SERVES 8

●

These stuffed chicken breasts are an incredibly easy and impressive dish to serve as part of a Mexican dinner or buffet.

1 pound ground chorizo sausage (bulk, or removed from casings if links)

4 ounces toasted pine nuts

1 bunch green onions, chopped

8 boneless, skinless chicken breast halves

1 tablespoon butter

2 tablespoons flour

½ cup whole milk (or cream)

½ cup chicken broth

12 ounces prepared salsa (like Pace Picante)

2 tablespoons chopped fresh cilantro leaves (or more to taste)

8 ounces sharp Cheddar cheese, grated

Preheat oven to 350 degrees.

In a medium skillet over medium-high heat, cook the sausage until no longer pink. Drain off the fat; return to the pan and add the pine nuts and onions. Set aside.

Flatten each chicken breast between two sheets of wax paper until 1/2 inch thick. Sprinkle with salt and pepper. Evenly divide the chorizo mixture between each breast, placing on one-half of the breast. Fold over the other half, and secure edges with toothpicks to seal. Set aside.

In a medium saucepan over low heat, melt the butter. Whisk in the flour and continue to cook, whisking constantly, for 3 minutes. Slowly whisk in the milk, then the broth. Bring to a simmer and continue cooking, stirring, until thickened and smooth. Remove from the heat and stir in the salsa. Season to taste with salt and pepper.

Pour 1/2 cup of the sauce into a 10x13-inch baking dish. Arrange stuffed chicken breasts on top of the sauce. Pour remaining sauce evenly over the top of the chicken. Sprinkle the top with chopped cilantro and shredded cheese. Bake for 45 minutes to 1 hour or until chicken is done (no longer pink and juices run clear).

MAKE AHEAD Dish can be prepared but not baked earlier in the day, covered and refrigerated. Bring to room temperature before baking.

Chicken Kiev

SERVES 6 TO 8

This dish was a favorite of both my brother Jim's and mine when we were kids. It was often requested for birthday dinners as we were always allowed to determine the menu (a birthday treat from Mom!).

¾ cup butter at room temperature (do not use margarine)
1 teaspoon dried tarragon
1 tablespoon chopped fresh parsley
½ teaspoon chopped garlic
½ teaspoon salt
¼ teaspoon ground white pepper
8 boneless, skinless chicken breast halves
¼ cup flour
2 eggs, beaten
1 cup fine bread crumbs
vegetable oil for deep fat frying

In a medium mixing bowl, thoroughly mash together the butter, tarragon, parsley, garlic, salt and pepper. Pat out the butter mixture on a piece of foil until you have a 4-inch square that is 1/2 inch thick. Wrap and freeze until firm, at least 30 minutes.

Place chicken breast, skinned side down, between several sheets of waxed paper. Pound with flat side of mallet until thin and even. Repeat with each chicken breast. Remove butter from the freezer and cut square into 12 sticks. Place one stick in the center of each chicken breast. Fold chicken over butter, enclose sides and roll up. Secure with toothpicks. Dip into flour to coat, then beaten egg, then bread crumbs. Chill for at least 30 minutes. Set aside remaining 4 sticks of herb butter.

Put a large amount of cooking oil into a deep, large dutch oven or deep fat fryer. Heat to 375 degrees. Fry 3 or 4 chicken breasts at a time—do not crowd. Cook for 4 or 5 minutes or until brown. Drain on paper towel; place each cooked breast on a dinner plate. Melt 4 sticks of herbed butter and pass on the side.

MAKE AHEAD Chicken breasts can be prepared up to the chilling stage up to 24 hours ahead, covered and kept in the refrigerator. Do not bring to room temperature before cooking. Once cooked, the chicken can be held in a 250 degree oven for around 1 hour (no more).

Roasted Chicken Sausage and Butternut Squash

SERVES 5 TO 6

●

This is a satisfying and flavorful dish that is perfect for when squash is in season and I'm trying to use the last of my garden herbs before the first snowfall. You can purchase a two-pound bag of peeled and cubed butternut squash at Costco, which reduces the prep time on this recipe to about five minutes!

2 pounds peeled, seeded and cubed (½ to ¾ inch) butternut squash (around 6 cups)

8 cooked chicken sausages (like chicken and apple), cut into ¾-inch pieces

4 teaspoons chopped garlic

1 tablespoon chopped fresh rosemary

1 tablespoon chopped fresh sage

1 tablespoon chopped fresh thyme

3 tablespoons roasted red pepper olive oil (can also use plain olive oil)

Preheat oven to 450 degrees.

In a large roasting pan, combine squash, sausage, garlic, rosemary, sage and thyme. Drizzle with oil, season with salt and pepper and toss to mix. Roast until squash is tender, stirring occasionally, for about 25 to 30 minutes.

Turkey and Spinach Enchiladas

SERVES 6

●

Another of Mom's delicious, last-minute dinners that is easy and quick to put together.

1 pound ground turkey

2 cups salsa, divided (we like Pace Picante)

1 package (10 ounce) frozen chopped spinach, thawed and squeezed dry

8 ounces cream cheese, cubed (can use regular or Neufchatel)

12 (6-inch) corn tortillas

1 can (14½ ounce) chopped tomatoes, undrained

1 teaspoon ground cumin

¾ cup shredded sharp Cheddar cheese

3 cups shredded lettuce

½ cup sour cream

Preheat oven to 350 degrees. Spray a 9x13-inch baking dish with cooking spray.

In a large nonstick skillet over medium heat, brown ground turkey, stirring constantly. Remove from heat and place in a food processor and process briefly, until meat is broken into crumbles. Put back into pan and add 1 cup salsa, spinach and cream cheese. Stir over medium heat until cheese melts. Remove from skillet, season to taste with salt and pepper, and set aside.

Wipe out skillet and heat over medium heat until hot. Spray both sides of a tortilla with cooking spray and place in skillet, cooking 15 seconds on each side. Spoon around 1/3 cup of turkey mixture in middle of tortilla; roll up and place seam side down in prepared dish. Repeat to make 12 enchiladas.

Combine remaining salsa, tomatoes and cumin and pour over top of enchiladas, spreading to cover entire enchilada. Sprinkle with salt and pepper. Bake for 25 to 30 minutes or until heated through. Sprinkle Cheddar on top and let stand until cheese starts to melt, about 2 minutes.

Place 1/2 cup lettuce on each dinner plate, top with two enchiladas and a tablespoon of sour cream.

MAKE AHEAD Enchiladas can be assembled but not baked earlier in the day, covered and refrigerated. Bring to room temperature before baking.

Spicy Turkey Meatloaf

My husband Robert loved this the first time I made it. There is just enough kick to it to make it interesting, without being too spicy.

MEATLOAF

1 can (7 ounce) chipotle chiles in
   adobo sauce
½ cup chopped onion
½ cup chopped fresh cilantro
¼ cup regular oats
¼ cup bread crumbs
¼ cup tomato sauce
2 teaspoons chopped fresh parsley
1 teaspoon salt
½ teaspoon ground cumin
½ teaspoon dried oregano
¼ teaspoon dried basil
¼ teaspoon ground black pepper
1 teaspoon chopped garlic
2 large egg whites
2 pounds ground turkey
   (mix of regular and breast)

TOPPING

¼ cup tomato sauce
1 tablespoon ketchup
½ teaspoon Tabasco

Preheat oven to 350 degrees. Spray a 9x5-inch loaf pan with cooking spray.

Place chipotle chiles and their sauce in a food processor and blend until puréed. In a large bowl, combine 4 to 5 teaspoons of the purée with remaining ingredients (onion through ground turkey). Mix well. Spoon mixture into prepared loaf pan and bake, uncovered, for 30 minutes.

Combine tomato sauce, ketchup and Tabasco. Brush mixture evenly over meatloaf, cover with foil and bake an additional 30 minutes or until thermometer registers 160 degrees. Let stand ten minutes before serving.

NOTE Keep leftover chipotle chile purée in a closed container in the refrigerator. It is excellent on sandwiches and in any sauce you want to spice up a bit with a smoky flavor. It lasts for months.

MAKE AHEAD Meatloaf can be prepared but not baked earlier in the day, covered and refrigerated. Bring to room temperature before serving.

meats

Steaks with Dijon, Caper and Green Onion Sauce page 110

It's no secret: the Claytons are meat eaters! Growing up in Colorado, we'd venture every summer to Wyoming to spend a week with the Gordon family at their ranch. Inspired by these trips, my brother Jim and I have recently started buying grass-fed beef, and we highly recommend it. Not only is it nutritionally better for you, it tastes fabulous. Since we can't eat beef every night, we're just as wild about pork and lamb. No matter, in our family, we often marinate, sear, grill, baste and roast our way to a fabulous dinner.

Steaks with Dijon, Caper and Green Onion Sauce

SERVES 6

In addition to complementing steak, this sauce serves beautifully alongside any red meat. You'll find that it's easy enough for everyday and elegant for entertaining. Round out the menu with Roasted Tomato and Arugula Salad and mashed potatoes. *(Photo, page 108)*

6 sirloin or rib-eye steaks
   (about 8 ounces each,
   ¾ inch thick)
½ cup olive oil
2 teaspoons red wine vinegar
2 teaspoons Dijon mustard
4 green onions, chopped
½ cup capers, drained

Preheat grill or broiler. Season steaks with salt and pepper and either grill or broil 4 inches from heat until desired doneness (about 6 to 8 minutes per side for medium).

While the steaks are cooking, whisk together the oil, vinegar and Dijon mustard in a small mixing bowl. Stir in the onions and capers. Season to taste with salt and pepper. Spoon sauce over cooked steaks or pass on the side.

MAKE AHEAD The sauce can be made several hours ahead, covered and kept at room temperature.

Mom's Steak and Lamb Marinade

FOR 1 FLANK STEAK OR LEG OF LAMB

●

Once you cook steak or lamb with this marinade, you won't want to make it any other way—just ask my friends Luisa and Cynthia!

½ cup vegetable oil
½ cup soy sauce
¼ cup sherry
2 teaspoons dry ginger
2 teaspoons dry mustard
1 large garlic clove, minced

Whisk all ingredients together in a shallow glass baking dish. Add flank steak or leg of lamb and marinate for at least 5 to 7 hours, preferably at room temperature. Remove from marinade and grill meat until medium rare.

VARIATION My brother Jim likes to substitute tequila for the sherry for a different flavor.

Mom's Favorite Beef Stroganoff

SERVES 4

Mom never found a beef stroganoff recipe that she liked better than this one. One taste of this delectable dish and you'll know why!

1½ pounds lean beef, cut into narrow strips around 2½ inches long
3 tablespoons butter, divided
1 cup sliced mushrooms
1 large yellow onion, peeled and thinly sliced
1 teaspoon chopped garlic
2 tablespoons flour
2 cups beef broth
3 tablespoons sherry
2 tablespoons tomato paste
1 teaspoon dry mustard
⅔ cup sour cream

Dust the strips of beef with salt and pepper; set aside for around 2 hours at room temperature.

In a large skillet over medium heat, melt 2 tablespoons of the butter and sauté the mushrooms until tender. Remove from the pan and set aside but do not clean out the pan. To the pan add the sliced onion and the garlic and cook, stirring occasionally, until the onion is soft and lightly browned. Remove and set aside. Add remaining 1 tablespoon of butter to the pan, increase heat to medium-high and once the butter is melted and hot, add the beef and sear on both sides, leaving the meat rare on the inside. Remove and set seared beef aside but do not clean out the pan.

Sprinkle the flour over the melted butter remaining in the pan, reduce heat to low and whisk the mixture for 2 to 3 minutes. Slowly whisk in the beef broth. Whisk in the sherry, tomato paste and dry mustard and cook until blended (just a minute or two). Stir in the meat, onions and mushrooms and simmer over low heat for around 20 minutes, stirring occasionally. Around 5 minutes before serving, stir in the sour cream. Serve over cooked white rice or egg noodles.

MAKE AHEAD Stroganoff can be made up to 24 hours ahead excluding the addition of the sour cream. Store covered and refrigerated. Reheat over medium heat just until warm, stir in sour cream and serve.

Veal Stroganoff

SERVES 4

This recipe was one of Mom's favorites not only because it's delicious, but it's a great way to serve veal inexpensively. Veal stew meat typically costs about a third the price of veal chops or scaloppini. The Italian sausage makes this dish especially flavorful. Mom thought that this dish tastes best served over egg noodles, but fettuccini makes for a more elegant presentation.

2 tablespoons vegetable oil

1½ pounds veal stew meat

3 mild uncooked Italian sausages (about 3 ounces each), casings removed and sliced into 1-inch pieces

1 medium yellow onion, chopped

½ pound mushrooms, quartered

1 cup beef broth

1 medium red bell pepper, seeded and chopped

½ cup dry sherry

6 to 8 ounces egg noodles

1 cup sour cream

2 tablespoons flour

Chopped fresh parsley for garnish

Heat oil in a large skillet over medium-high heat. Add veal and sausage meat and cook, stirring occasionally, until well browned. Add onion and mushrooms and cook until onion is soft. Stir in broth, bell pepper and sherry. Bring to a boil; cover, reduce heat and simmer for about 1 hour or until the meat is tender.

After the veal mixture has been cooking for about 45 minutes, add 2 quarts of water to a large stock pot and bring to a boil. When the meat is done (tender), drop the egg noodles into the boiling water and cook for 5 to 6 minutes or until desired doneness. Drain and rinse with hot water. Set aside.

Whisk together the sour cream and flour and gently stir into the veal mixture until well blended. Continue cooking just until heated through. Season to taste with salt and pepper.

Place a portion of egg noodles on each serving plate. Top with veal mixture. Sprinkle chopped parsley on the top.

MAKE AHEAD The stroganoff and noodles can be cooked up to 4 hours before serving, and stored separately, covered, in the refrigerator. Reheat the stroganoff in a large skillet over medium heat. Bring 2 quarts of water to a boil and drop in the cooked noodles for no more than 30 seconds, just to reheat.

This hearty meal is ideal for a cold fall or winter evening. Mom always insisted that you must use "good quality" red wine to maximize the flavor. Mashed potatoes serve as a scrumptious side dish.

3 tablespoons vegetable oil, divided

1¼ to 1½ pounds cubed beef (often labeled "beef for stew")

1 medium white onion, chopped

1 large carrot, peeled and chopped

1 large celery rib, chopped

½ to ¾ teaspoon bouquet garni*

1½ cups good quality Burgundy red wine

3 tablespoons butter at room temperature, divided

1½ cups sliced mushrooms

1½ tablespoons flour

1 tablespoon chopped fresh parsley

* Available in the spice section of most grocery stores, bouquet garni is a mixture of several dried, chopped herbs.

In a large Dutch oven, heat 2 tablespoons of the vegetable oil over medium-high heat until hot. Wipe any moisture off of the beef and sauté in the oil, stirring occasionally, until browned (around 5 minutes).

With a slotted spoon, remove the beef to another dish and set aside, leaving any accumulated juices in the pan. Add the chopped onion, carrots and celery to the pan and cook for 5 to 7 minutes, until beginning to soften and most of the juice from the meat is cooked out. Put the beef back in the pan. Season with salt and pepper and stir in the bouquet garni and red wine. Bring to a boil, reduce heat, cover and simmer over very low heat for 2 1/2 to 3 hours, stirring occasionally.

Shortly before serving, melt the remaining 1 tablespoon oil and half the butter (1 1/2 tablespoons) in a medium frying pan over medium-high heat. When hot, sauté the mushrooms until softened and slightly browned (5 to 7 minutes). Set aside.

Mix the remaining 1 1/2 tablespoons butter and flour together to form a paste. When the stew is done, add the flour mixture and stir until well blended. Continue to cook until thickened (doesn't take long). Stir in the mushrooms and cook for a few minutes to blend the flavors. Garnish with fresh parsley and serve immediately.

MAKE AHEAD The Boeuf Bourguignon can be made through the simmering step up to one day ahead. Cover and store in the refrigerator. Reheat before continuing with the remaining steps.

Bobotee

SERVES 4 TO 6

●

Mom and Dad frequently traveled internationally and fortunately my brother Jim and I often got to go along. As a result, we were exposed to many wonderful dishes and Mom's collection of international recipes was incredibly diverse and interesting. After a trip to South Africa, she served this South African version of meatloaf at dinner parties and Dad showed slides from the trip. With an eclectic combination of ingredients, Bobotee is delicious!

2 tablespoons butter
1 large yellow onion, chopped
1 tart apple, peeled, cored and diced (Granny Smith works well)
1 tablespoon curry powder, or more depending on the strength of your curry powder
2 pounds extra lean ground beef, or a combination of 1 pound beef and 1 pound ground lamb
½ cup dry bread crumbs
2 eggs, divided
1½ cups whole milk, divided
2 tablespoons red wine vinegar
2 tablespoons apricot jam
2 teaspoons salt
¼ teaspoon fresh ground pepper
½ cup toasted slivered almonds
6 bay leaves

Preheat oven to 350 degrees.

In a large skillet or sauté pan, melt the butter over medium-high heat. Sauté the onion and apple until soft, around 10 minutes. Stir in curry powder and cook for 1 additional minute. Place in a large mixing bowl and add the ground beef, bread crumbs, 1 beaten egg, 1/2 cup of the milk, vinegar, apricot jam, salt, pepper and almonds. Mix well by hand and pack into a 7x11-inch baking dish. Arrange bay leaves on top and bake for 50 minutes.

In a small mixing bowl, whisk together the remaining egg and 1 cup milk. Remove bay leaves, drain off some of the excess grease if there is a lot (you won't need to do this unless you are using all beef) and slowly pour milk mixture over the meatloaf. Bake for an additional 10 minutes.

MAKE AHEAD Bobotee can be assembled but not baked earlier in the day, covered and refrigerated. Bring to room temperature before cooking.

Evie's Enchilada Pie

SERVES 6 TO 8

●

Among our friends, this dish is known as "the moving casserole." Years ago, my roommate at the time, Katey Hartwell, and I endured a tough move in the middle of a major Denver snowstorm. After the movers delivered the last of the furniture, our friend Don Greco came along with this Enchilada Pie for dinner. For Katey and me, it was the best meal we'd ever eaten! Since that day, it is now a tradition among our close friends for someone to deliver this casserole on moving day along with margaritas. More often than not, it turns into the first party in the new home as everyone wants a helping of Enchilada Pie!

1 pound ground beef
1 medium yellow onion, chopped
1 garlic clove, minced
1 can (7 ounce) diced green chiles, drained
1 can (10.5 ounce) golden mushroom soup, undiluted
1 can (4 ounce) mushroom stems and pieces, drained
1 can (16 ounce) Mexican stewed tomatoes, undrained
½ teaspoon chili powder
½ cup picante sauce
tortilla chips (Nacho cheese flavor)
1 pound grated Cheddar cheese
guacamole, salsa, sour cream for serving

Preheat oven to 350 degrees. Spray a 9x13-inch glass baking dish with cooking spray.

In a large skillet, cook the ground beef, onion and garlic until the beef is cooked through and lightly browned. Drain off grease and stir in the green chiles, golden mushroom soup, mushroom stems and pieces, tomatoes, chili powder, and picante sauce. Season to taste with salt and pepper. Simmer 10 to 15 minutes.

Line baking dish generously with tortilla chips. Stand large chips up straight along sides of pan. Spoon beef mixture evenly over the chips. Top with grated cheese. Crumble a few tortilla chips on top. Cover loosely with foil and bake for 45 to 60 minutes. Let sit for 5 minutes before serving. Serve with guacamole, salsa and sour cream on the side.

MAKE AHEAD Casserole can be assembled but not baked earlier in the day, covered and refrigerated. Bring to room temperature before baking.

Korean Barbeque Beef

SERVES 3 TO 4

●

We can always count on cousin Dave Berry for a delectable recipe. This one is a personal favorite for its wonderful blend of flavors. We like to serve it over brown rice.

1½ to 2 tablespoons grated
    fresh ginger
1 cup chopped yellow onion
⅓ cup chopped fresh cilantro
1 teaspoon chopped garlic
1 tablespoon sesame seeds
2 tablespoons brown sugar
¼ cup soy sauce
3 tablespoons sesame oil
Dash oyster sauce
Dash Tabasco sauce
1 pound flank steak, sliced thinly
    across the grain and cut in
    half crosswise

In a 7x11-inch glass baking dish, stir together all ingredients except the steak. Add the steak slices and stir to coat the meat. Cover and marinate in the refrigerator for at least 2 hours, stirring occasionally.

Remove the steak slices from the marinade, letting the excess drip back into the dish, reserving the marinade. Heat a large skillet over medium heat. Add the steak and cook, covered for around 10 minutes or until the meat is cooked, stirring occasionally. Stir in the reserved marinade, uncover, reduce the heat to medium-low and simmer for 10 to 15 minutes.

Sally's Corned Beef and Cabbage
SERVES 6

Every year, we were treated to Mom's distinctive corned beef and cabbage for St. Patrick's Day. Her recipe is consistently good and brings out the Irish in everyone!

3 pounds corned beef brisket
2 medium yellow onions, sliced
1 teaspoon chopped garlic
6 whole cloves
2 bay leaves
6 small white potatoes, peeled
6 small (but not baby) carrots, peeled and cut into 3" pieces
1 medium cabbage, cut into 6 wedges
Dijon mustard
¼ cup brown sugar
¼ teaspoon ground cloves

Place corned beef, onions, garlic, whole cloves and bay leaves in large Dutch oven. Cover with water, cover and simmer on a stovetop for 3 hours (one hour per pound) or until fork tender.

Preheat oven to 350 degrees.

Remove meat from liquid and set aside, leaving cooking liquid and spices in the pan. Add the potatoes and carrots to the pan. Cover, bring to a boil and cook for 10 minutes. Add the cabbage wedges and cook for an additional 20 minutes or until the vegetables are done.

While the vegetables are cooking, spread the Dijon mustard on the fat side of the meat. Mix together the brown sugar and cloves and sprinkle over the top, pressing down to adhere to the mustard. Place beef in a shallow baking pan and bake for 20 minutes or until top is nicely glazed.

Slice beef and serve with potatoes, carrots and cabbage on the side.

Fall-Off-the-Bone Slow Cooker Short Ribs

SERVES 4 TO 5

●

These ribs are so tender you practically don't need a knife to eat them—the meat just pulls apart with a fork. The sauce is very subtle and just enhances the flavor of the beef. Serve with Creamy Parmesan Polenta for a real comfort food meal.

1 medium yellow onion, chopped
½ teaspoon chopped garlic
1 cup ketchup
¼ cup light brown sugar
3 tablespoons Worcestershire sauce
1 teaspoon salt
2 teaspoons Dijon mustard
3 pounds beef short ribs (bone-in)

Whisk together the onion, garlic, ketchup, brown sugar, Worcestershire sauce, salt, mustard and 1/2 cup water. Set aside.

If needed, cut the ribs into individual pieces (one bone per piece). Place in the bottom of a slow cooker. Pour the onion mixture over the top, covering completely. Cover and heat on low for 4 to 6 hours (the longer the better!). Depending on the fattiness of your beef, you may need to spoon off some grease before serving. Serve the extra sauce on the side.

Barbequed Lamb Chops

SERVES 8

●

Busy weeknights call for quick delicious dinners. These grilled lamb chops fit the bill perfectly. Serve with Grilled Vegetable Packets and a tossed green salad.

1 cup dry red wine
½ cup extra virgin olive oil
2 green onions, chopped
1 teaspoon chopped garlic
1 tablespoon chopped
  fresh parsley
1 tablespoon chopped
  fresh rosemary
1 tablespoon fresh thyme leaves
1 tablespoon chopped
  fresh oregano
1 teaspoon salt
¼ teaspoon fresh ground pepper
6 large lamb loin chops
  (about 1 inch thick)

In a medium mixing bowl, whisk together the wine, olive oil, onions, garlic, herbs, salt and pepper. Place lamb chops in a shallow baking dish. Pour marinade over and lift up chops to ensure marinade coats both sides. Cover and refrigerate for at least 12 hours, preferably overnight, turning occasionally.

Grill chops over medium-high heat about 4 inches from the heat, for 4 to 5 minutes per side, until internal temperature reaches 140 degrees, for medium to medium rare. Let sit for 2 to 3 minutes before serving.

Clayton Lamb Curry

SERVES 4 - 6

The Clayton family loves curry. And, this recipe is a winner by a mile. The sweet and spicy flavors blend together incredibly well. An added bonus is that it freezes beautifully (without the rice or condiments) to savor later.

2 tablespoons extra virgin olive oil
1 apple, cored, peeled & chopped
1 green pepper, chopped
2 medium yellow onions, chopped
1 garlic clove, crushed
2 tablespoons flour
1 tablespoon curry powder
½ teaspoon salt
½ teaspoon dried marjoram
½ teaspoon dried thyme
1 cup consommé or beef broth
½ cup dry red wine
½ lemon
½ cup raisins
2 whole cloves
2 cups diced cooked lamb
¼ cup shredded coconut (optional)
1 tablespoon sour cream

CONDIMENTS
Crumbled bacon
Chopped hard boiled eggs
Raisins
Coconut
Mango chutney
Chopped green onions
Chopped pineapple
Chopped cashews

In a large skillet, heat olive oil over medium-high heat and sauté apple, green pepper, onion and garlic until onions are soft. Sprinkle flour, curry powder, salt, marjoram and thyme over mixture in skillet, mix well and stir constantly over medium heat for 5 minutes. Add consommé or beef broth, red wine, juice from 1/2 lemon, raisins and cloves. Simmer for 20 to 30 minutes. Add lamb (and coconut if using) and cook for an additional 15 minutes until heated through. Stir in sour cream just before serving. Serve with cooked white rice and condiments.

MAKE AHEAD Curry can be made up to 24 hours ahead excluding the addition of the sour cream. Store covered and refrigerated. Reheat over medium heat just until warm, stir in sour cream and serve.

Rack of Lamb with Nut Crust

SERVES 8

●

Rack of lamb is really very easy to make and so impressive at a dinner party. People often steer away from lamb because not everyone likes it, but in all my years of entertaining only one person who has come to dinner wasn't a fan. So I say—go for it!

1 cup ground hazelnuts

1 cup fresh bread crumbs, preferably made from French bread

3 tablespoons chopped fresh rosemary

5 racks of lamb (8 ribs each), trimmed by the butcher

3 tablespoons Dijon mustard

Preheat oven to 425 degrees.

Combine hazelnuts, bread crumbs and rosemary in a medium mixing bowl. Place racks of lamb on large rimmed cookie sheets, meat side up. Brush with mustard. Season with salt and pepper. Press breadcrumb mixture onto Dijon mustard.

Roast for about 25 minutes or until a meat thermometer inserted into the thickest part of a rack registers 130 degrees (for medium-rare, the best way to serve lamb). Let racks stand outside the oven for 10 minutes. Cut between each rib to separate and serve.

Country Ham

●

Country ham is another traditional food from Kentucky adopted by our family. Mom served it not only on Derby day but also at every major holiday celebration.

Country ham ordered from Smith's Country Store in Cave City, Kentucky (270.773.3530)

Rub down the ham with a towel to get some of the salt off. Immerse the ham completely in water (we like to put it in a sealed garbage bag filled with water, inside a cooler, surrounded by ice). Let the ham soak for at least 2 and up to 12 hours (but no more). If you want a less salty ham, soak it for the longer time and change the water a couple of times. You can also add 1/2 cup vinegar to the water.

Drain the ham and place it fat side up in a large roasting pan. Cover it with as much water as will fit in the pan. Most likely about 1/5 of the ham will be above the water. Place it on the lower rack of a cool oven, and turn the oven on to 300 degrees. Roast it for 6 hours, turning it over after 2 to 3 hours. Wiggle the bone—when it's loose, the ham is done. Drain, cool and remove the layer of fat. Slice into thin serving pieces. Ham will keep for several days in the refrigerator.

NOTE Pieces on the ends of the ham can get tough. I chop them in a food processor and use the chopped ham as a garnish just like bacon bits—in salads, on pasta, in casserole dishes. Mom used to mix it with cream cheese for a spread with crackers. Cousin Jim Kidwell mixes 1/2 cup of the chopped ham with 3 tablespoons mayonnaise, 1 tablespoon mustard, and 1 teaspoon (or more to taste) horseradish for another spread.

Roast Pork Loin with Plum Conserves

SERVES 8

●

This is a wonderful make-ahead entrée that works all year around. I have served it as part of a summer garden party and also at a Christmas party buffet. Everyone loves the combination of the mustard and pork with the plum conserves. Substitute peaches for the plums if you prefer.

PORK LOIN
3 to 4 pounds boneless pork loin
1½ teaspoon chopped garlic
¾ cup coarse grain mustard

PLUM CONSERVES
1 pound fresh plums, pitted
   and chopped
1½ cups sugar
¾ cup raisins
1 tablespoon grated orange rind
¼ cup fresh orange juice
¼ cup chopped walnuts

Preheat oven to 375 degrees.

Place the pork loin on a rack in a shallow roasting pan. Mix together the garlic and mustard and spread a thick layer over the outside of the loin. Sprinkle with fresh ground pepper. Bake for 30 to 35 minutes per pound, or until the internal temperature reaches 155 to 160 degrees. Remove the meat from the oven, bring to room temperature, then cover and place in the refrigerator to chill for at least 2 hours before serving.

While the pork is cooking, make the conserves. In a large saucepan, combine the plums, sugar, raisins, 1/4 cup water and orange rind. Bring to a boil, reduce heat and simmer for 20 minutes. Add the orange juice and continue simmering for another 10 minutes. Stir in the walnuts and simmer for another 5 minutes. Remove from the heat, cool, then cover and place in the refrigerator to chill for at least 2 hours before serving.

To serve, place the conserves in a bowl in the middle of a large platter. Surround with slices of the pork. Best if served at room temperature.

NOTE When doubling this recipe, put the garlic and mustard mixture onto the pork loin halfway through cooking time as it takes longer to cook. That way the coating won't burn.

MAKE AHEAD The conserves can be made up to one week in advance and stored, covered, in the refrigerator. The pork can be made up to one day in advance and also stored, covered, in the refrigerator.

Pork Tenderloin with Port, Balsamic and Cranberry Sauce

SERVES 4

●

Enjoy this versatile dish for an everyday dinner or a fancier occasion. Consider wild rice as an accompaniment.

½ cup dried cranberries
1 teaspoon canola oil
2 pork tenderloins
   (around 1¼ pounds total)
1 shallot, minced
½ cup port
¼ cup balsamic vinegar
1 cup chicken broth
½ teaspoon dried thyme
1 teaspoon cornstarch

In a small saucepan, combine the dried cranberries and 1 cup water. Bring to a boil, reduce heat and simmer for 3 minutes. Drain, reserving both fruit and cooking liquid. Set aside.

Slice the pork tenderloin into 16 medallions. Heat the oil in a large nonstick skillet over medium heat. Season the pork with salt and pepper and add to the skillet. Cook until browned on the outside and no longer pink inside, about 3 minutes per side. Transfer to a serving platter, cover and keep warm. (Do not wash the skillet.)

In the same skillet, add the shallots and cook over medium heat, stirring, for 30 seconds. Add the port and vinegar and bring to a boil, stirring to scrape up any browned bits on the bottom of the skillet. Boil until reduced by half, around 3 to 5 minutes. Add chicken broth, thyme and the reserved cranberry cooking liquid; boil until reduced again by half, around 5 to 7 minutes.

In a small bowl, dissolve the cornstarch with 1 tablespoon water. Whisk the cornstarch mixture into the sauce and cook, stirring, until slightly thickened and glossy. Stir in the reserved cranberries and season to taste with salt and pepper. Spoon the sauce over the pork medallions on the serving platter and serve immediately.

VARIATION You can also place 4 pork medallions on individual serving plates and top with the sauce.

Pork Tenderloin Stuffed with Spinach and Cheese
SERVES 4 TO 6

●

This recipe was one of the fortunate outcomes of an evening where I was rummaging in the refrigerator looking to cook with items I had on hand. After combining three different recipes, the result was surprisingly good—easy enough for everyday and attractive enough for entertaining. If you don't have all the ingredients, start with the spinach and let your pantry and refrigerator be your guide.

1 tablespoon olive oil

2 teaspoons chopped garlic, divided

3 tablespoons chopped sun-dried tomatoes packed in oil, drained (more to taste)

3 tablespoons chopped green onion

1 teaspoon lemon zest

2 packages (10 ounce) frozen chopped spinach, thawed, drained and squeezed dry

1 cup goat cheese crumbles

2 pork tenderloins (around ¾ pound each)

2 tablespoons fresh lemon juice

4 teaspoons Dijon mustard

Preheat the oven to 375 degrees.

Heat the olive oil a large skillet over medium heat. When hot, add 1 teaspoon of the chopped garlic and sauté for just a minute. Add the sun-dried tomatoes, green onion, lemon zest and spinach. Cook, stirring, until heated through and any moisture remaining on the spinach is cooked out. Turn heat to low and add goat cheese and keep stirring until the cheese is well incorporated and begins to melt. Season with salt and pepper and remove from heat.

Place one pork tenderloin on a large cutting board and cut it in half length-wise, cutting mostly but not all the way through. Open it up so the tenderloin lies flat in one piece. Cover with wax paper and pound to an even thickness. Trim off tail ends so the tenderloin is a rectangular shape. Repeat with second tenderloin.

Season the pork with salt and pepper. Take half of the spinach mixture and spread it in the middle of one tenderloin. Fold up the sides and secure with toothpicks. (Note: if you have pounded your tenderloin fairly thin, you may want to roll it up instead of folding it, and secure it by tying the tenderloin up with string.) Repeat with second tenderloin. Place side by side in a 7x11-inch baking dish. You may have some filling left over, depending on the size of your tenderloins.

In a small bowl, whisk together the remaining garlic, lemon juice and Dijon mustard. Brush over the top and sides of the stuffed tenderloins. Bake until the tenderloins reach 155 to 160 degrees with an instant-read thermometer, approximately 50 minutes (make sure you are measuring the temperature of the tenderloins and not the stuffing).

Remove to a cutting board and with a sharp knife carefully cut into 1-inch slices. Remove toothpicks after cutting.

MAKE AHEAD Pork can be stuffed but not baked earlier in the day, covered and refrigerated. Bring to room temperature before baking.

A well-seasoned memory

Mom's style of entertaining was built around generous hospitality and her goal was always to have ample food for everyone. At one of her earliest dinner parties she served Cornish game hen— evidently a big hit, because before everyone had gone through the buffet line, it was clear that she was short on hens. Live and learn, but vowing that would never happen again, if she saw people taking more than she had anticipated, she would announce "FHB!" We all knew the code for Family Hold Back, and Dad, my brother and I took smaller portions to ensure our guests had enough!

Sally celebrating another successful dinner.

Grilled Pork Tenderloin with Ginger Couscous

SERVES 8

●

The beauty of this dish is that it's a complete dinner that suits a summer or early fall get-together.

PORK TENDERLOIN

4 pork tenderloins (¾ to 1 pound each)
½ cup soy sauce
¼ cup dry sherry
3 tablespoons honey
2 tablespoons grated fresh ginger
1 teaspoon chopped garlic

GINGER COUSCOUS

3½ cups chicken broth
3 tablespoons rice vinegar
1 tablespoon honey
1½ tablespoons chopped fresh ginger
½ teaspoon dry mustard
2 cups couscous
1 pound Chinese pea pods (frozen)

Trim silvery membrane and any fat from tenderloins. Fold thin end of each tenderloin under to make meat evenly thick; tie to secure. Place meat in a ziploc baggie (may need 2 depending on the size of your tenderloins). In a small mixing bowl, whisk together the soy sauce, sherry, honey, ginger and garlic. Pour into baggie with meat, seal and refrigerate at least 30 minutes or up to 24 hours, turning occasionally.

Remove meat from marinade, and place marinade in a small bowl. Grill meat over medium heat, covered, turning occasionally to brown evenly. Brush frequently with the marinade. Cook until the meat at the thickest part registers 150 to 155 degrees on a meat thermometer, around 15 to 20 minutes. Remove from heat, let sit for 5 to 10 minutes, then slice.

Meanwhile, in a large saucepan, bring the chicken broth to a boil over high heat. Add the vinegar, honey, ginger and mustard. Stir in couscous. Cover and remove from the heat. Let stand 10 minutes or until the liquid is absorbed. Stir with a fork to fluff, and let stand, uncovered, at room temperature until ready to use (if making more than a few hours ahead, cover and store in the refrigerator).

While the meat and couscous are cooking, cook the pea pods according to package directions. Drain and set aside.

Place couscous mixture either on a serving platter or individual dinner plates. Top with pea pods, then sliced pork.

MAKE AHEAD The pea pods and the couscous can be prepared up to one day ahead and stored, covered, in the refrigerator. Bring to room temperature before serving.

Pork and Green Bean Sauté

SERVES 4

●

Recipes that incorporate the entrée, starch and vegetable make weeknight cooking easy and flavorful. This pork tenderloin and its accompaniments fit the bill.

¼ cup soy sauce (regular or low sodium)

2 teaspoons cornstarch

1 pound pork tenderloin, cut into ¼-inch slices

1 pound green beans, cut into bite-size pieces (you should have 4 cups)

2 teaspoons dark sesame oil

1 to 2 tablespoons chopped fresh ginger

1 teaspoon chopped garlic

¼ cup chicken broth (regular or fat-free)

2 cups hot cooked rice (optional)

¼ cup chopped toasted cashews

Combine the soy sauce and cornstarch in a medium bowl; add pork slices, tossing to coat. Cover and place in the refrigerator to marinate for at least 15 minutes. Steam beans until crisp-tender. Remove from heat and plunge into ice water. Drain well.

Heat sesame oil over medium-high heat in a large nonstick skillet or stir-fry pan coated with cooking spray. Add ginger and garlic; sauté 1 minute. Add pork and its sauce and stir for 1 or 2 minutes. Add green beans and stir another few minutes until the pork is done. Stir in chicken broth, reduce heat and simmer for 2 minutes. Serve over hot rice and garnish with chopped cashews.

Chinese Stir-Fry Ground Pork and Eggplant

SERVES 4

●

An ex-pat friend gave this recipe to me while we were both living in Amsterdam. In the U.S., you can find all the ingredients at Whole Foods, a gourmet shop or ethnic food store.

½ pound ground pork
2 tablespoons soy sauce, divided
1 tablespoon dry sherry
2 tablespoons vegetable oil
1½ teaspoons bean sauce
1½ teaspoons oriental chili sauce
2 garlic cloves, chopped
1 teaspoon fresh ginger, minced
½ teaspoon salt
1¼ pounds Asian eggplants,
   cut into ½-inch dice (can
   use regular eggplant)
1 tablespoons sugar
½ cup chicken broth
2 teaspoons cornstarch
1 tablespoon balsamic vinegar
1 teaspoon dark sesame oil
2 teaspoons sesame seeds,
   toasted
2 green onions, finely chopped

In a bowl, mix together the pork with 1 tablespoon of soy sauce and the sherry. In a stir-fry pan, heat the vegetable oil over high heat until smoking. Add the chili-bean sauce, garlic, ginger and salt and cook over high heat for 30 seconds. Add the ground pork and cook, stirring until browned, 2 to 3 minutes, breaking up the meat into pieces. Add the eggplant and stir until it begins to soften, about 3 to 4 minutes. Add the sugar and the remaining 1 tablespoon of soy sauce and cook, stirring, for about 30 more seconds. Stir in the broth, cover, reduce heat to medium and cook until the eggplant is tender, about 10 minutes.

Mix the cornstarch with 2 tablespoons water. Stir the vinegar and the cornstarch mixture into the pork mixture and keep stirring until the sauce thickens, which should happen quickly. Remove from the heat and stir in sesame oil, sesame seeds and green onion. Serve immediately with brown or white rice.

VARIATION For a prettier presentation, after the sauce has thickened, transfer the stir-fry to a serving platter or individual serving plates. Drizzle the top with the sesame oil and sprinkle with the sesame seeds and green onion.

Dijon Pork Chops with Arugula

SERVES 4

●

This dish is perfect for dinner in a jiffy. These chops have a nice, tangy flavor and don't require any advanced marinating.

¼ cup red wine vinegar
¼ cup extra virgin olive oil
2 tablespoons Dijon mustard
1 tablespoon chopped fresh
   parsley
1½ teaspoons chopped fresh
   chives
1½ teaspoons chopped fresh
   tarragon
4 boneless pork chop loins,
   1 inch thick
1 bunch arugula, cleaned and
   stems removed
Extra virgin olive oil

Preheat grill or broiler.

In a small bowl, whisk together the vinegar, oil, mustard, parsley, chives and tarragon. Place chops on grill or broiler pan and brush top liberally with mustard mixture. Cook for 8 to 10 minutes (over medium heat if on grill), turn and brush again with mustard mixture. Cook an additional 8 to 10 minutes or until done (when the chops reach around 160 degrees on an instant-read thermometer). Watch carefully—they will dry out if overcooked.

While the chops are cooking, toss the arugula with enough olive oil to coat. Season with salt and pepper to taste. Serve on top or to the side of the pork chops.

Cajun Pork Chops

SERVES 4

This recipe is so simple yet delicious, with just the right amount of spice. I like to pre-mix these seasonings and keep them in a small jar with my spices so they are ready to go the next time I want to make this recipe. Note that you can also grill these chops if you prefer.

1 tablespoon paprika
½ teaspoon ground cumin
½ teaspoon sage
½ teaspoon ground pepper
½ teaspoon garlic powder
½ teaspoon cayenne pepper
½ tablespoon butter
½ tablespoon vegetable oil
4 boneless center-cut pork chops, around ½ inch thick

Combine paprika, cumin, sage, pepper, garlic powder and cayenne on a plate or in a shallow bowl. Coat chops with seasoning mixture on both sides. Lightly sprinkle with salt.

Heat butter and oil over high heat in a large skillet until hot (almost smoking). Place chops in skillet, reduce heat to medium and cook 3 to 4 minutes. (Use a splatter screen!) Flip chops and cook an additional 3 to 4 minutes until done.

VARIATION Grill the chops over medium heat for around 4 to 5 minutes per side, or until the internal temperature reaches 155 degrees on an instant read thermometer. Allow to sit for 5 minutes before serving.

Sausage and Spinach Torte

This dish is fabulous for a picnic or tailgating. Serve it with a French baguette and a variety of mustards and cheeses—*mais oui! (Photo, page 6)*

1 pound bulk pork sausage, mild or hot (to your taste—we like hot)
1 medium yellow onion, chopped
⅓ cup fresh French bread crumbs
¼ cup whole milk
1 package (10 ounce) frozen chopped spinach
1 cup freshly grated Parmesan cheese
3 eggs, beaten
1 teaspoon salt
½ teaspoon ground black pepper
½ teaspoon dried sage
½ teaspoon grated nutmeg

Preheat the oven to 350 degrees. Butter a 9x5-inch loaf pan.

In a medium skillet over medium-high heat, cook the sausage, stirring, just until no longer red. Break the sausage into pieces as it cooks. Add the onion and cook, stirring, until the onions are lightly golden and the sausage is cooked through, about 10 minutes. Set aside to cool slightly. Put meat mixture in a food processor and mince. Place in a large mixing bowl and stir in the bread crumbs and milk. Set aside.

Thaw the frozen spinach, drain and squeeze dry in paper towel. Add the spinach to the meat mixture and stir in the cheese, eggs, salt, pepper, sage and nutmeg. Spoon the mixture into the prepared pan and bake, uncovered, for 50 minutes or until set. Cool, cover and chill. Bring to room temperature before serving with a variety of mustards.

MAKE AHEAD Torte can be made up to 2 days in advance.

seafood and fish

Salmon with Crumb Topping and Herb Mayonnaise **page 141**

Mom loved to cook and experiment with recipes. As a result, my brother Jim and I were exposed to many new and different foods. Adding to our gastronomic good fortune, we grew up near the Granada Fish Market, one of the best fishmongers in Denver, at a time when access to fresh fish and seafood was limited in the middle of the country. Today, from fresh to frozen, there is an almost unlimited variety of fish and seafood available at virtually every grocer and specialty store. If you don't make many fish entrées or want to expand your horizons, there's never been a better time than now to dive right in.

Mascarpone and Spinach Stuffed Salmon

SERVES 8

Stuffed entrées make impressive presentations, and they often are surprisingly easy to prepare—just like this salmon. Mom liked to serve this at a spring or summer dinner party.

1 package (10 ounce) frozen chopped spinach
4 ounces cream cheese at room temperature
½ cup mascarpone cheese at room temperature
Pinch ground nutmeg
8 salmon fillets, skin on, (6 to 8 ounces each, about 1 inch thick)
2⅔ cups fresh French bread crumbs
½ cup butter, melted
½ cup freshly grated Parmesan cheese

Preheat oven to 450 degrees. Brush a rimmed baking sheet with olive oil.

Thaw spinach under running hot water. Drain, squeeze dry and place in a medium mixing bowl. Mix in cream cheese, mascarpone and ground nutmeg. Season to taste with salt and pepper. Set aside.

Make a cut in the center of the top side of each salmon fillet—making sure not to cut through the skin or all the way to the ends. This will create a shallow pocket. Fill each pocket with an equal portion of the spinach mixture.

Place the fillets, skin side down, on the prepared baking sheet and season with salt and pepper. Mix bread crumbs, melted butter and Parmesan cheese in a medium bowl. Top each fillet with the bread crumb mixture, pressing down to adhere. Bake until salmon is opaque in the center, about 12 minutes. Transfer to plates and serve immediately.

MAKE AHEAD Salmon fillets can be stuffed earlier in the day, covered and refrigerated.

Salmon with Crumb Topping and Herb Mayonnaise

SERVES 6 TO 8

●

Mom and I have both been serving this salmon at dinner parties for years. It is very easy as all the prep work can be done the day before. Without fail, every time we serve it, someone asks for the recipe. Sure enough, a couple of months later we are at someone else's dinner party eating this salmon! *(Photo, page 138)*

HERB MAYONNAISE
⅓ cup chopped fresh Italian parsley
⅓ cup chopped fresh cilantro
¼ cup chopped green onions
2 tablespoons red wine vinegar
½ teaspoon chopped garlic
½ teaspoon dried oregano
¼ teaspoon freshly ground
   black pepper
⅛ teaspoon cayenne pepper
1 cup mayonnaise

SALMON
½ cup chopped fresh Italian parsley
¼ cup freshly grated Parmesan
   cheese (or more to taste)
¼ cup chopped fresh thyme
2 teaspoons lemon zest
½ teaspoon salt
2 teaspoons chopped garlic
2 to 2¼ cups fresh bread crumbs
½ cup butter, melted
2½-pound salmon fillet
   (in one piece)

Preheat oven to 350 degrees. Butter a shallow baking pan large enough to hold the fish.

To make the herb mayonnaise: in a medium mixing bowl, stir together the parsley, cilantro, onions, vinegar, garlic, oregano and peppers. Stir in mayonnaise. Cover and refrigerate until ready to use.

To make the crumb topping for the salmon: place the parsley, Parmesan cheese, thyme, lemon zest, salt and garlic in the bowl of a food processor and process until finely chopped and mixed together. Transfer to a medium mixing bowl and mix in bread crumbs (we like to do this by hand).

Place the salmon skin side down in the prepared pan. Pat the bread crumb mixture over the top. Drizzle the melted butter evenly over the bread crumbs. Bake fish until desired doneness, around 20 minutes. Serve with mayonnaise mixture on the side.

MAKE AHEAD The mayonnaise and crumb mixture can be made the day before, covered and refrigerated. Bring both to room temperature before using.

Salmon and Summer Vegetables en Papillote
SERVES 4

•

We love cooking fish *en papillote,* which simply means wrapping it in a parchment paper or foil package and then baking it. You can also cook fish this way on the grill. For this recipe, you can use any combination of the vegetables you like or that are in season.

6 tablespoons fresh orange juice
¼ cup hoisin sauce
1 teaspoon chopped garlic
4 salmon fillets, around
　6 ounces each
½ pound fresh asparagus
½ pound zucchini
½ pound yellow squash
½ pound carrots
2 teaspoons orange zest

Preheat oven to 425 degrees.

In a dish large enough to hold the salmon fillets in one layer, whisk together the orange juice, hoisin sauce and chopped garlic. Add salmon, turning it to coat, cover and refrigerate for at least 30 minutes and up to 4 hours.

Discard tough ends of asparagus. Cut off tips and set aside. Cut stalks in half lengthwise and then in half crosswise, to form matchsticks that are around 2 to 3 inches long. Place in a large mixing bowl; add the asparagus tips. Set aside.

Cut the ends off of the zucchini. Cut the zucchini in half crosswise, then cut each piece into matchsticks that are around 2 to 3 inches long. Add to the asparagus. Repeat process with the yellow squash and carrots. Toss the mixture to combine.

Tear off four 24-inch long pieces of parchment paper or foil. (Note that if you are grilling, you won't want to use parchment paper.) Mound 1/4 of the vegetables in the center of one piece of foil. Top with one salmon fillet. Repeat process 3 more times. Sprinkle top of each fillet with 1/2 teaspoon orange zest. Drizzle the marinade over the top of the salmon. Season fish and vegetables with salt and pepper. Draw together two opposite edges of the paper or foil and fold over to seal. Fold ends under and seal. Place packets in one layer on a large cookie sheet and bake for 15 minutes or to desired tenderness. Remove from oven and open carefully as the steam will be hot. Transfer salmon and vegetables to a serving platter or individual plates, drizzling cooking liquid from inside the packets over the top.

VARIATION Place prepared foil packets on a preheated grill over medium heat and cook for around 15 to 20 minutes.

Baked Halibut with Tomatoes and Capers with a Feta-Crumb Crust

SERVES 6

●

This dish takes a bit longer to prepare than most in this cookbook, but this recipe is so delicious we just had to include it!

HALIBUT
6 tablespoons extra virgin olive oil, divided

3 cups thinly sliced white onion

2 tablespoons thinly slivered garlic (can also use chopped)

1 cup thinly sliced fennel bulb

4 anchovies, rinsed and finely minced

2 tablespoons chopped fresh parsley

3 pounds ripe plum tomatoes, peeled, seeded and diced (can also use 3 cups diced and drained canned Italian tomatoes)

2½ pounds fresh halibut, cut into 1-inch pieces

¼ cup chopped fresh basil

3 tablespoons small capers, rinsed and drained

¼ cup dry red wine

⅓ cup grated Parmesan cheese

CRUST
½ cup crumbled feta cheese

3 tablespoons chopped pine nuts

½ cup dry bread crumbs (we like to use Panko)

1 tablespoons fresh thyme (lemon thyme, if available)

Preheat oven to 350 degrees. Lightly oil a 3-quart baking dish with 2 tablespoons of the olive oil.

In a sauté pan or large skillet, heat 3 tablespoons of the olive oil and sauté the onions, garlic and fennel until softened but not brown. Add the anchovies and parsley and cook 2 minutes more. Remove from heat and spread half of the onion mixture in the bottom of the prepared baking dish. Scatter half the tomatoes on top and season with salt and pepper. Arrange the fish pieces evenly over the top of the tomatoes and scatter the basil and capers on top. Season again with salt and pepper. Drizzle with the red wine. Layer on the remaining half of the onion mixture, followed by the remaining tomatoes. Sprinkle the Parmesan cheese on top.

Finely crumble the feta cheese and drain on paper towels, if necessary. In a medium mixing bowl, combine the feta, pine nuts, bread crumbs, thyme and remaining 1 tablespoon olive oil. Scatter evenly over the top of the casserole. Bake for 30 to 35 minutes or until the fish is done and the topping is a light golden brown.

MAKE AHEAD The casserole can be assembled but not baked earlier in the day, covered and refrigerated. Increase cooking time to 40 to 45 minutes.

Grilled Tuna with Puttanesca Sauce

SERVES 4

●

With this recipe, you can have a delicious, flavorful dish on the table in minutes.

¾ cup chopped fresh tomatoes
⅓ cup chopped olives–black or green
1 to 2 tablespoons capers
2 teaspoons chopped garlic
1 teaspoon fresh lemon juice
1 teaspoon anchovy paste
⅛ teaspoon red pepper flakes
1 teaspoon dried oregano
4 tuna steaks, ¾ inch thick

Preheat grill.

In a medium bowl, stir together the tomatoes, olives, capers, garlic, lemon juice, anchovy paste, red pepper flakes and oregano. Season to taste with salt and pepper. Set aside.

Season tuna steaks with salt and pepper and grill over medium heat for 4 minutes on each side or until desired doneness. Serve with sauce on top or on the side.

Grilled Mustard-Tarragon Swordfish

SERVES 4

A fabulous blend of flavors. So easy, yet so delicious! Serve with Green Beans with Lemon-Butter Sauce and a tossed salad.

2 tablespoons + 1 teaspoon freshly squeezed lemon juice (about ½ lemon), divided
2 tablespoons mayonnaise
4 tablespoons sour cream
4 teaspoons Dijon mustard
1 tablespoon chopped fresh tarragon
1½ pounds Swordfish (can also use halibut or tuna)
½ teaspoon capers, drained

Preheat grill.

In a small bowl, mix together the 2 tablespoons lemon juice, mayonnaise, sour cream, Dijon mustard and tarragon. Season to taste with salt and pepper. Set aside.

Spray grill rack with non-stick cooking spray. Sprinkle remaining 1 teaspoon lemon juice on one side of fish. Grill, lemon juice side up, for 4 minutes over medium heat. Turn over. Spread top with mayonnaise mixture. Grill for approximately 6 minutes, or until fish is done. Remove to serving plate and sprinkle with capers.

ALTERNATE VERSION You can use 6 tablespoons of mayonnaise and omit the sour cream.

Asian Swordfish

SERVES 4

●

This recipe comes from my longtime friend Cynthia Ballantyne. It's delectable on a hot summer evening served with Roasted Asparagus, Brown Rice Gratin and a tossed salad.

6 tablespoons vegetable oil
3 tablespoons soy sauce
2 tablespoons dry sherry
1½ teaspoons peeled and grated or finely chopped ginger root
1 teaspoon grated orange rind
4 swordfish steaks (6 ounces each)

In a small mixing bowl, whisk together first five ingredients. Place the fish steaks in a glass baking dish large enough to hold all four. Pour marinade over the top, cover and marinate in the refrigerator for at least 2 hours and up to 6 hours. Turn occasionally.

Preheat grill. Spray grill rack with non-stick cooking spray. Remove steaks from marinade and grill over medium hot coals for around 4 minutes per side, then turn over and continue grilling for another 3 to 4 minutes, or until desired doneness. (Remember that the fish will continue cooking after you remove it from the grill, so we like to take it off when it is slightly underdone.)

A well-seasoned memory

●

Sometimes a little cooking rivalry results in the grandest meals. After I graduated from college, Mom and Dad, my college roommate Cynthia and I went to Hilton Head where we stayed at a family friend's home. About halfway through our vacation, Mom's older brother Dan drove up from Ft. Lauderdale to join us. Dan loved to cook just about as much as Mom did. Within 24 hours of Uncle Dan's arrival, the beach house turned into the site for a Lee family cook-off. For the remainder of the week, we were treated to the most amazing meals. While Mom and Dan were vying for the title of top family chef, Dad, Cynthia and I were the real winners of that friendly feast competition!

Mom planning her next gathering.

Baked Fish on Lettuce

SERVES 6

●

This recipe has been around for many years, yet I still have friends who ask for it when they come to dinner. Despite its simplicity, it's very impressive looking, especially if you bake it in an attractive pan. The original recipe called for red snapper but since that fish is now on the warning list of fish to avoid, we suggest using halibut or tilapia instead.

4 cups shredded iceberg lettuce
2 pounds red snapper, tilapia or
  halibut fillets
1 cup mayonnaise
1 cup freshly grated Parmesan
  cheese
2 green onions, chopped
Chopped parsley

Preheat oven to 350 degrees. Grease a baking dish large enough to hold the fish fillets in one layer (preferably one that can double as a serving dish).

Cover the bottom of the prepared dish with the shredded lettuce. Place the fish on top of the lettuce. If using individual fillets instead of one large piece, you can slightly overlap the fillets to fit them in the pan.

In a medium bowl, mix together the mayonnaise, Parmesan and onions. Season with salt and pepper to taste. Spread the mixture evenly on top of the snapper. Bake for 30 minutes or until the fish is cooked through and the topping is lightly browned. Sprinkle with chopped parsley and serve.

Tilapia with Mushrooms and Tarragon

SERVES 8

You can use any medium-density, flaky fish for this recipe, including cod, flounder, halibut or snapper.

½ cup butter, divided
16 ounces sliced mushrooms
½ cup flour
4 cups whole milk
3 tablespoons chopped fresh
    tarragon
½ teaspoon ground white pepper
⅔ cup dry white wine
1 cup grated Parmesan cheese
8 tilapia steaks (6 to 8 ounces
    each), rinsed and dried
1 tablespoon chopped fresh
    parsley

Preheat oven to 350 degrees. Butter a 9x13-inch baking dish.

Melt 1 tablespoon butter in a large frying pan over medium-high heat. Add mushrooms and cook, stirring frequently, until mushrooms are lightly browned, about 8 to 10 minutes. Reduce heat to medium-low and add remaining butter and then the flour. Cook, stirring, until bubbling, about 2 minutes. Gradually stir in milk, tarragon and pepper; stir until sauce boils. Stir in wine and Parmesan. Season to taste with salt. Remove from heat.

Arrange fish in the prepared pan in a single layer. Pour sauce over fish. Bake, uncovered, until fish is opaque in the thickest part, 15 to 20 minutes. Test fish after 10 minutes to make sure not to overcook. Sprinkle parsley over the top and serve.

MAKE AHEAD Dish can be assembled but not baked earlier in the day, covered, and refrigerated. Bring to room temperature before cooking.

Fish Substitutions

Sometimes when there's a fish recipe I want to make, my local store doesn't have the fish called for. I find the following guideline helpful in determining what's fresh and available for substituting. (Your fishmonger can also suggest substitutes.)

GROUP 1: THIN AND DELICATE
Sole
Flounder

GROUP 2: MEDIUM-DENSE AND FLAKY

Lean, mild flavor
Striped bass
Cod
Haddock
Flounder
Halibut (California)
Lingcod
Perch
Pike
Rockfish
Snapper
Tilapia
Tilefish

Moderately lean, mild flavor
Catfish
Salmon
Sea bream
New Zealand snapper
Sea trout
Rainbow and brown trout

Oilier
Carp
Greenland turbot
Lake trout
Black cod
Butterfish
Chilean sea bass
Shad
Whitefish

Distinctively flavored
Barracuda
Herring
Sardines
Mackerel
Striped mullet
Pompano
Salmon

GROUP 3: MEDIUM-DENSE, EXTRA-FIRM FLAKES
Drum
Mahi mahi
Orange roughy
Papio (Hawaiian jack)
Sea bass (white)

GROUP 4: DENSE AND MEATY

Lean, mild flavor
Grouper
Halibut (Northern, Alaska)
Sea bass (bluenose and Hawaiian)
New Zealand sea bream
Shark

Moderately lean to oilier, distinctively flavored
Cobia
Jack
Amberjack
Yellowtail
Mackerel
Sturgeon
Swordfish
Tuna

Baked Shrimp with Tomato, Feta Cheese and Capers

SERVES 4

●

This recipe is a family favorite that Mom, my cousin Beth and her husband Jim, and I have being serving to rave reviews for years. It works equally well for a large crowd or an intimate gathering. Beth and Jim once served it to a party of 50, and I've served it to my bridge group. It's perfect either way because all the prep can be done in advance.

3 cups canned Italian plum
   tomatoes (preferably imported),
   undrained—around 3 cans
¼ cup bottled clam juice
1 teaspoon dried oregano
1 teaspoon dried red pepper flakes
2 tablespoons capers, drained
¼ cup olive oil
3 tablespoons butter
1 teaspoon chopped garlic
1 pound uncooked medium shrimp,
   shelled and deveined
¼ pound feta cheese, crumbled

Preheat oven to 350 degrees.

In a large saucepan over medium-high heat, bring the tomatoes (undrained) to a boil and cook until reduced to around 2 cups (around 15 minutes). Cut the tomato pieces up with scissors while cooking if too large. Stir often to prevent sticking and burning. Add the clam juice, oregano, pepper flakes, capers and salt and pepper to taste. Set aside.

In a large skillet, heat the olive oil and butter. Add garlic and shrimp and cook briefly, 1 to 2 minutes, stirring until shrimp are pink. Set aside.

Spoon equal portions of tomato sauce (about 1/2 cup) into each of four large ramekins and spoon shrimp mixture (including butter sauce they cooked in) on top. Sprinkle crumbled feta cheese over the top. Place ramekins on a large rimmed cookie sheet and bake for 10 to 15 minutes or until bubbly and hot. Remove from oven and serve immediately.

VARIATION Cousin Jim Kidwell likes to substitute one can of chopped tomatoes with green chiles or jalapeños, to add a little spice to this dish.

MAKE AHEAD Ramekins can be assembled earlier in the day and refrigerated. Bring to room temperature before baking.

Shrimp with Sherry-Bread Crumb Topping

SERVES 4 TO 6, DEPENDING ON SIZE OF SHRIMP

●

This simple and savory recipe can be on the table in mere minutes.

2 pounds shrimp, cooked and shelled
1 shallot
2 tablespoons capers, drained
½ cup butter, melted
½ cup dry sherry
2 teaspoons chopped fresh tarragon
½ teaspoon dried marjoram
1 cup fresh bread crumbs
⅓ cup chopped fresh parsley

Preheat oven to 400 degrees. Butter the sides and bottom of a shallow baking dish large enough to hold the shrimp in one layer.

Spread the shrimp in the bottom of the prepared pan.

Finely chop the shallot. In a small bowl, mix together the chopped shallot, capers, melted butter, sherry, tarragon and marjoram. Stir in bread crumbs and blend well. Season to taste with salt and pepper. Spread the bread crumb mixture over the top of the shrimp; sprinkle top with the chopped parsley. Bake for 25 to 30 minutes or just until hot; make sure not to overcook or the shrimp will get tough. Serve immediately.

VARIATION IN COOKING METHOD If all you have is raw shrimp, or you prefer your bread crumb topping to be crunchy, use the same ingredients but follow these directions:

Sauté raw, shelled shrimp in 3 to 4 tablespoons of melted butter (and chopped garlic to taste, if you like) just until done.

While the shrimp are cooking, finely chop the shallot. In a small bowl, mix together the chopped shallot, capers, melted butter, sherry, tarragon and marjoram. Stir in bread crumbs and chopped parsley and blend well. Season to taste with salt and pepper. Put bread crumb mixture in a medium skillet and cook over medium-high heat, stirring constantly, until mixture begins to brown slightly.

Put shrimp in a serving dish, or on individual serving plates, and sprinkle hot bread crumb mixture over the top, pouring over any melted butter that may remain in the skillet. Serve immediately.

Shrimp Tostadas

SERVES 4

In 2007, Robert and I were invited to a local benefit where corn tortillas were being made from scratch during dinner. At the end of the evening, I noticed that most of the bread baskets on the tables were close to full, so to Robert's embarrassment, I filled my purse and the pockets of his tuxedo with the leftover tortillas. After making various enchilada recipes with them, I decided to experiment and came up with this shrimp dish, which both Robert and I love. You don't have to rob a bread basket for your tortillas—they taste good with store-bought, too! *(Photo, page 2)*

½ cup extra virgin olive oil, divided

8 corn tortillas (best if you can find homemade)

1 cup sliced mushrooms

¾ cup sliced yellow onion

4 teaspoons Mexican seasoning (or more to taste)

24 ounces cooked small shrimp (not cocktail size)

½ cup salsa-flavored cream cheese*

½ cup prepared guacamole

½ cup shredded Monterey Jack or other mild, white cheese

½ cup purchased chunky-style salsa

1 cup shredded lettuce

* Available at Whole Foods. If you can't find it in your area, you can substitute plain cream cheese spread (in a tub) or mix together ½ cup cream cheese spread with 1 tablespoon of salsa.

Heat 1/4 cup olive oil in a small skillet over high heat until very hot. Add one corn tortilla and cook until starting to crisp (about 1 minute); use tongs and turn over. Cook just until crispy. Place on paper towel to drain. Repeat with remaining tortillas.

Heat the remaining 1/4 cup olive oil in a medium skillet over medium heat until hot. Add the mushrooms and onion; stir in Mexican seasoning. Cook, stirring occasionally, until mushrooms and onion are soft. Stir in shrimp and cook just until the shrimp are heated through and seasoned. Add more Mexican seasoning and salt to taste.

While the mushroom and onion mixture is cooking, spread 1 tablespoon of the cream cheese on each cooked tortilla. Top with 1 tablespoon of the guacamole. When the mushrooms, onion and shrimp are done, place equal amounts on top of each tortilla and top with shredded cheese, salsa and lettuce.

NOTE To make your own Mexican seasoning, combine together 1/2 cup chili powder, 1/4 cup paprika, 2 tablespoons ground cumin, 2 teaspoons garlic powder, 1 teaspoon cayenne pepper, and 1/2 teaspoon salt. Store in an airtight jar (this is the seasoning used in our Black Bean Chicken Enchiladas).

Shrimp and Sausage Gumbo
SERVES 10

This flavorful dish was another of Mom's favorites. It's so easy to make and always a crowd pleaser.

½ cup butter

1 package (10 ounce) frozen cut okra

1 can (15 ounce) diced tomatoes, undrained

½ green bell pepper, finely chopped

2 medium onions, finely chopped

2 tablespoons flour

1 cup beef broth or stock

½ teaspoon chopped garlic

1 can (8 ounce) tomato sauce

4 teaspoons Worcestershire sauce

⅛ teaspoon dried basil

1 bay leaf

½ teaspoon cayenne pepper

½ teaspoon chili powder

⅛ teaspoon ground cloves

¼ teaspoon oregano

⅛ teaspoon ground black pepper

2 pounds medium shrimp, peeled and deveined

1 pound andouille sausage, sliced

In a large stock pot, melt the butter over medium heat. Add the okra, tomatoes and their juice, green pepper and onion and sauté until the onion is soft and transparent, around 10 minutes. Stir in the flour and cook another 3 minutes. Gradually stir in the beef broth and continue cooking, stirring, until thickened. Add the garlic, tomato sauce, Worcestershire sauce and all the spices. Simmer, covered, for 35 minutes. Season to taste with salt and pepper. Add the shrimp and sausage and cook for an additional 7 to 10 minutes or until the shrimp are cooked through and sausage is hot. Serve over white rice.

MAKE AHEAD Gumbo can be prepared without adding the shrimp and sausage up to 24 hours ahead, covered and refrigerated. Reheat to a low simmer, add the shrimp and sausage and cook until the shrimp are cooked through and the sausage is hot.

Sautéed Shrimp and Cheese Grits
SERVES 6

●

Every kitchen can use a little southern hospitality! Shrimp and grits is a classic southern combination. Given our family's southern heritage—and my maternal grandmother's love of grits—we had to include this recipe in our book!

CHEESE GRITS

3 cups water
¼ teaspoon salt
1 cup quick-cooking grits
1 can (12 ounce) evaporated milk
2 tablespoons butter
½ teaspoon chopped garlic
3 ounces cream cheese, cubed
¼ cup chopped fresh parsley
2 tablespoons chopped fresh chives

SAUTÉED SHRIMP

1 tablespoon cornstarch
½ cup white wine
2 tablespoons butter
1½ pounds fresh large shrimp, peeled
1 tablespoon chopped fresh basil
1 tablespoon chopped fresh thyme
1 tablespoon chopped fresh chives
1 garlic clove, minced
¼ cup chicken broth (or seafood stock)

First, start preparing the grits: In a large saucepan, bring the water and salt to a boil. Slowly stir in the grits, then stir in the evaporated milk. Bring to a slow boil, reduce the heat to medium-low (so it is barely simmering) and cook for 10 minutes, stirring frequently.

While the grits are cooking, prepare the shrimp: In a small bowl, mix the cornstarch with the wine. Set aside. Melt the butter in a large non-stick skillet over medium heat. Add the shrimp, basil, thyme, chives and garlic. Sauté for 2 to 3 minutes, then add the chicken broth. When the shrimp start to turn pink, add the wine mixture. Continue cooking until the shrimp are cooked through, around another minute or so. Season with salt and pepper to taste.

When the shrimp are almost done, the grits should be finished cooking (at the end of the 10 minutes noted above). Stir the butter, garlic and cream cheese into the grits. Once melted, stir in the parsley and chives. Season to taste with salt and pepper. Serve shrimp and sauce over the cheese grits.

Scallops with Shallot Butter and Pine Nuts

SERVES 6

●

An easy and impressive main dish for entertaining. Scallops were one of Mom's favorites.

1¼ pounds bay or small sea scallops, rinsed and drained

12 tablespoons butter at room temperature

3 tablespoons finely chopped shallots

2 tablespoons pine nuts

1 tablespoon chopped fresh parsley

½ cup fresh bread crumbs

1 tablespoon fresh lemon juice

Preheat oven to 450 degrees. Lightly grease six scallop shells or large ramekins.

Divide scallops evenly among prepared dishes. In a medium mixing bowl, using your hands, work together the butter, shallots, nuts, parsley, bread crumbs and lemon juice. Spread equal amounts with the back of a moistened spoon over top of scallops. Don't worry if it doesn't cover all of the scallops; the butter will spread out as it melts. Place dishes on a rimmed baking sheet and bake for 10 minutes or until piping hot and bubbly. Note that they will continue cooking when you take them out of the oven so be careful not to overcook.

MAKE AHEAD The scallops can be prepared but not baked earlier in the day. Cover with plastic wrap and store in the refrigerator. Bring to room temperature before baking.

Baked Crab and Mushroom Casserole

SERVES 6

●

Mom had been making this recipe for years, and it is just as pleasing today as it was 40 years ago. A great make-ahead meal, this casserole can be frozen until ready to use. You can substitute imitation crabmeat, but it tastes best with the real thing (and canned is fine).

9 tablespoons butter, divided
16 ounces sliced mushrooms
⅓ cup flour
1 can (10 ounce) chicken broth
1½ cups light cream
½ cup bread crumbs
1½ pounds fresh lump crabmeat
1 cup grated American cheese

Preheat oven to 350 degrees. Butter a 7x11-inch baking dish.

In a large skillet over medium heat, melt 2 tablespoons of the butter. Sauté the mushrooms until tender, about 5 minutes. Remove mushrooms from pan and set aside. Do not clean the pan.

In the same pan over low heat, melt 6 tablespoons of the butter. Slowly whisk in the flour, and cook for 3 minutes, whisking constantly. Slowly whisk in the chicken broth, then the cream. Bring to a slow boil, stirring constantly, and cook until thickened. Season with salt and pepper to taste.

In the microwave, melt the remaining 1 tablespoon of butter and toss together with the bread crumbs. Set aside.

Spread 1/2 of the mushrooms over the bottom of the prepared dish. Top with 1/2 of the crab, 1/2 of the cheese and 1/2 of the cream sauce. Repeat layers. Sprinkle the bread crumbs over the top. Bake the casserole for about 30 minutes or until bubbly and lightly browned.

MAKE AHEAD The casserole can be assembled, but not baked, and frozen. To serve, put frozen casserole in 325 degree oven and bake for about 45 to 60 minutes, or until bubbly and lightly browned on top.

pasta

Pesto Chicken and Vegetable Fettuccine **page 162**

Lately, because we and so many of our friends are watching our diets and cutting down on carbohydrates, we don't seem to be eating as much pasta as we used to. So, when we sit down for pasta meal, we make it special and treat ourselves. My pasta recipes are a collection of our family favorites.

Pesto Chicken and Vegetable Fettuccine

SERVES 4

●

I make a large batch of pesto in late July or August, when the basil in my herb pot is abundant. I keep it in a closed jar in the refrigerator and it lasts for months! Store-bought pesto works equally well. You'll find this dish is a perfect mid-week, late summer supper as it comes together quickly. *(Photo, page 160)*

1 medium red bell pepper
1 medium yellow bell pepper
½ pound asparagus, trimmed
1 tablespoon extra virgin olive oil
1 thinly sliced yellow onion
3½ cups chopped, cooked chicken
4 teaspoons chopped sun-dried
    tomatoes (packed in oil), drained
¾ cup pesto, divided
6 tablespoons freshly grated
    Parmesan cheese, divided
1 pound fettuccine

Bring a large pot of salted water to a boil for the pasta.

In the meantime, core, seed and slice the bell peppers into thin strips and cut into 1-inch pieces. Cut the asparagus into 1-inch pieces. In a large skillet, heat the olive oil until hot and sauté the peppers, asparagus and onion over medium-high heat until softened but still crisp, about 10 minutes. Transfer to a large mixing bowl and add the chicken and sun-dried tomatoes. Toss with 1/2 cup of the pesto and 2 tablespoons of the Parmesan cheese. Season with salt and pepper to taste.

Once the water boils, cook the fettuccine *al dente*. Drain, return to the pot and toss with the remaining pesto and 2 tablespoons of the Parmesan cheese. Season with salt and pepper to taste.

Mound the fettuccine on a large serving dish (or 4 individual serving plates) and top with the chicken and vegetable mixture. Sprinkle with the remaining 2 tablespoons Parmesan cheese (or more to taste). Serve immediately.

Cajun Shrimp Linguine

SERVES 4

A wonderfully flavorful pasta dish that isn't too spicy.

8 ounces dry linguine
1 tablespoon extra virgin olive oil
¾ teaspoon chopped garlic
(or more to taste)
¼ cup chopped green onions
2 teaspoons dried Cajun seasoning
1 can (12 ounce) evaporated skim
milk
¼ teaspoon Worcestershire sauce
¼ teaspoon Tabasco sauce
½ cup grated Parmesan cheese
(plus more for serving)
12 ounces shelled, cooked
medium-size shrimp

Cook the linguine according to package directions, until *al dente*. Drain in a colander and rinse under hot water. Set aside.

While the pasta is cooking, heat the oil in a large nonstick skillet over medium-high heat. When hot, add the garlic and cook just until it sizzles (around 1 minute). Stir in the green onions and Cajun seasoning and cook for 1 minute. Stir in the milk, bring to a boil, reduce heat to low and simmer for 5 minutes. Stir in the Worcestershire sauce, Tabasco, and 1/4 cup of the Parmesan cheese. Simmer for 3 minutes. Stir in the shrimp and pasta and heat for 2 to 3 minutes, just until the shrimp is heated through. Remove from the heat and stir in the remaining Parmesan. Season to taste with salt and pepper.

Serve immediately, passing more Parmesan cheese on the side.

Salmon Linguine in a Vermouth Cream Sauce

SERVES 4

Vermouth accents the wonderful blend of flavors in this pasta dish. Serve with a side salad and fresh Italian bread.

1 cup whipping cream
½ cup dry vermouth
¼ cup soy sauce
12 ounces dried linguine
3 tablespoons extra virgin olive oil
1 teaspoon chopped garlic
2 medium shallots, chopped
12 sun-dried tomatoes packed in oil, drained and chopped
¾ cup chopped fresh basil
2 cups sugar snap peas or Chinese pea pods, cut in half
1 pound fresh salmon fillet, skinned, boned and cut into small bite-size pieces
1 cup walnuts, roasted and chopped
½ cup grated Parmesan cheese

In a small bowl, whisk together the cream, vermouth and soy sauce. Set aside.

Cook the linguine according to package directions until *al dente*. Drain in a colander and rinse under hot water.

While the pasta is cooking, heat a large sauté pan over high heat. When hot, add the olive oil, garlic and shallots and stir. When the garlic begins to sizzle (should only take around 15 seconds) stir in the tomatoes, basil and peas. Continue stirring for 1 minute, then slowly pour in the cream mixture. Bring to a boil, then add the salmon. Cook until salmon is almost done, carefully stirring (should only take about 1 minute). Add the cooked pasta and walnuts and toss the mixture to combine. Remove from the heat and toss with the Parmesan. Season with salt and pepper to taste. Serve immediately.

Spinach and Cheese Penne

SERVES 6 TO 8

●

This recipe is a snap to put together and is also a delicious vegetarian entrée.

12 ounces uncooked, dry penne
   pasta
1 tablespoon extra virgin olive oil
½ cup chopped onion
1 teaspoon chopped garlic
3 cups prepared spaghetti sauce
   (1 24-ounce jar)
½ teaspoon crushed red pepper
   flakes
¾ cup cottage cheese
½ cup ricotta cheese
¼ cup fresh grated Parmesan
   cheese
1 egg, beaten
1 package (10 ounce) frozen
   chopped spinach, thawed,
   drained and squeezed dry
1 cup shredded mozzarella cheese
   (or to taste)

Preheat oven to 350 degrees. Spray a 9x13-inch baking dish with nonstick cooking spray.

Cook the penne according to the package directions for *al dente*. Drain, rinse, and drain again. Set aside.

In medium saucepan, heat the olive oil over medium heat. Add the onions and garlic and cook until the onions are soft, about 4 minutes. Add the spaghetti sauce and red pepper. Bring sauce to a boil, reduce heat and simmer for 5 minutes, stirring occasionally. Remove from heat and set aside.

In a large mixing bowl, stir together the cottage cheese, ricotta cheese, Parmesan cheese and egg. Stir in the spinach. Season to taste with salt and pepper. Stir in the cooked penne and mix well.

Spread 1/2 cup of the red sauce over the bottom of the prepared pan. Top with half of the penne mixture. Pour half of the sauce that is left (around 1 1/4 cups) over the top, then half of the mozzarella cheese (1/2 cup). Repeat layers—the rest of penne mixture, then the rest of sauce and cheese. Cover and bake for 30 minutes.

MAKE AHEAD Dish can be made earlier in the day, covered and refrigerated. Bring to room temperature before baking.

Baked Farfalle with Prosciutto, Mushrooms and Cheese

SERVES 8 TO 10

●

While this dish isn't as quick and easy as some of the others, it isn't difficult. It does take about an hour to prepare but it's worth the extra effort. The good news is that it can be made ahead.

1 pound dried farfalle (bow tie) pasta

2 tablespoons extra virgin olive oil

2 cups chopped yellow onion

½ teaspoon chopped garlic

¼ teaspoon dried red pepper flakes

1 tablespoon chopped fresh basil

1 tablespoon chopped fresh oregano

1 pound fresh shiitake mushrooms, stems discarded and caps sliced

¼ cup unsalted butter, divided

3 tablespoons flour

2 cups whole milk

2 cans (28 ounce) Italian tomatoes (chopped if you can find them), drained well

¼ pound thinly sliced prosciutto, chopped

1 cup grated Italian Fontina cheese

1 cup Gorgonzola cheese crumbles

1½ cups freshly grated Parmesan cheese, divided

⅔ cup chopped fresh parsley

Preheat oven to 450 degrees. Butter a shallow 4-quart baking dish and set aside.

Fill a large pot with enough water to cook the pasta and bring it to a boil. Add the pasta and cook for 5 minutes—note that it will not be done—and drain well. Set aside.

While the water is boiling and pasta is cooking, heat the olive oil in a large skillet over medium-low heat and cook the onion, garlic, pepper flakes, basil and oregano until the onion is soft, stirring occasionally. Add the sliced mushrooms, turn the heat up to medium, and cook the mixture, stirring, until the mushrooms are tender (about 15 minutes). Transfer mixture to a large mixing bowl and don't wash out the skillet.

In the same skillet, melt 3 tablespoons of the butter over low heat, whisk in the flour and cook, stirring, for 3 minutes. Slowly add the milk, whisking until incorporated. Increase the heat and bring the mixture to a slow boil, stirring frequently, and cook until thickened. Stir the sauce into the mushroom mixture. Add the tomatoes (chop them first if they aren't already chopped), prosciutto, Fontina and Gorgonzola cheeses, 1 1/4 cups of the Parmesan cheese and the parsley. Stir until well combined.

Add the cooked pasta to the mushroom and cheese mixture along with salt and pepper to taste and stir until well combined. Transfer the mixture to the prepared baking dish. Sprinkle the top with the remaining 1/4 cup Parmesan. Cut the remaining tablespoon of butter into small pieces and scatter over the top. Bake for 25 to 30 minutes, or until the top is golden brown and the pasta is tender.

MAKE AHEAD The casserole can be assembled but not baked up to 24 hours ahead, covered, and refrigerated. Bring to room temperature before baking.

Spinach Farfalle Bolognese

SERVES 10 TO 12

When we were growing up, all our relatives on Dad's side of the family came to our house for Christmas Eve dinner. Mom always made this dish because she could make it ahead and enjoy her time with family. Everyone, from little kids to grandparents, loved it.

½ pound bulk Italian pork sausage
1 pound lean ground beef
1 large yellow onion, chopped
½ teaspoon chopped garlic
1 can (15 ounce) tomato sauce
1 can (6 ounce) tomato paste
1 cup dry red wine
¾ teaspoon chopped fresh
   rosemary
¾ teaspoon chopped fresh basil
¾ teaspoon chopped fresh oregano
¼ teaspoon dried marjoram
¼ teaspoon savory
8 to 10 ounces dried farfalle
   (bow tie) pasta
2 packages (10 ounce) frozen
   chopped spinach, thawed and
   squeezed dry
2 cups sour cream
1½ cups grated Parmesan cheese

Preheat oven to 375 degrees.

Crumble sausage and ground beef in a large nonstick skillet and cook over medium-high heat until meat is no longer pink, stirring and breaking up meat into small pieces. Add onion and garlic and continue cooking, stirring frequently, until onion is soft. Stir in tomato sauce, tomato paste, red wine, 1/2 cup water, and seasonings (rosemary through savory). Bring to a boil; immediately reduce to low and simmer, uncovered, for about 30 minutes. Season to taste with salt and pepper.

While Bolognese sauce is simmering, cook the pasta according to package directions. Drain. In a medium bowl, mix together the spinach and sour cream. Mix cooked pasta with Bolognese sauce. Spread half of the mixture over the bottom of a 2 1/2- to 3-quart casserole dish. Dot the top with half of the spinach-sour cream mixture and spread to make an even layer. Sprinkle with half of the cheese. Repeat the layers and top with the remaining cheese. Bake, uncovered, for 40 to 50 minutes or until heated through and lightly browned on top.

MAKE AHEAD Can be prepared but not baked up to 24 hours in advance, covered and refrigerated. Bring to room temperature before baking.

Turkey Stuffed Pasta Shells

SERVES 4

●

Easy to make, impressive to serve and delicious to eat.

12 to 15 jumbo macaroni shells
8 ounces ground turkey
  (or chicken) sausage
1 cup finely chopped carrot
1 cup finely chopped zucchini
1 cup finely chopped red or
  green pepper
¼ cup finely chopped onion
4 ounces cream cheese, cut
  into squares
1 tablespoon chopped fresh basil
1½ teaspoons chopped fresh dill
¼ teaspoon garlic powder
1½ cups spaghetti sauce
¼ cup grated Parmesan cheese

Preheat oven to 350 degrees. Spray an 8-inch baking dish with nonstick cooking spray.

Cook pasta according to package directions; drain and set aside.

While the pasta is cooking, spray a large skillet with nonstick cooking spray and place over medium heat. Add the turkey sausage, carrot, zucchini, pepper and onion and cook for 7 to 8 minutes or until the sausage is no longer pink and the veggies are tender. Drain off fat. Reduce heat to low and stir in cream cheese, basil, dill and garlic powder and keep stirring until combined and the cheese is melted. Season to taste with salt and pepper. Remove from heat.

Spoon about 3 tablespoons of turkey mixture into each pasta shell and arrange, filled side up, in prepared dish. Pour spaghetti sauce over the top. Bake, covered, for 30 to 40 minutes or until hot. Sprinkle with Parmesan cheese before serving.

MAKE AHEAD Shells can be prepared but not baked earlier in the day, covered and refrigerated. Bring to room temperature before cooking.

Mexican Chicken Lasagna

SERVES 8 TO 10

This was one of Mom's favorite recipes for casual entertaining. You can make it up to one day ahead, and it is an unusual combination of flavors—we have never seen another Mexican-flavored lasagna.

2 tablespoons vegetable oil
½ teaspoon chopped garlic
1 medium onion, chopped
1 medium red bell pepper, seeded and chopped
2 jars (16 ounce) salsa (mild or medium, to taste – we like Pace Picante)
½ teaspoon ground pepper
2 tablespoons chili powder
1 teaspoon ground cumin
2 cups small curd cottage cheese
2 eggs, beaten
⅓ cup chopped fresh parsley
1 can (4 ounce) diced green chiles
1 package (10 ounce) no-boil lasagna noodles
4 cups chopped cooked chicken
1 cup shredded sharp Cheddar cheese
1 cup shredded Monterey Jack cheese

Preheat oven to 375 degrees.

Heat oil in a large sauce pan over medium heat. Add the garlic, onion and bell pepper and cook until limp, around 10 minutes. Add the salsa, pepper, chili powder and cumin. Bring to a boil, reduce heat and simmer, uncovered, stirring often, for around 10 minutes, or until the sauce is reduced to 4 cups. Season to taste with salt and pepper.

While the sauce is cooking, in a medium mixing bowl combine the cottage cheese, eggs, parsley and green chiles. Set aside.

Arrange half of the lasagna noodles in the bottom of a 9x13-inch baking dish. Carefully spread half of the cottage cheese mixture over the top. Top with half of the chicken. Spoon half of the sauce over the chicken, then sprinkle with half of the cheeses. Repeat layers—noodles, cottage cheese mixture, chicken, sauce, cheeses. Bake, covered, for 45 to 50 minutes, or until heated through. Let stand, uncovered, for 5 to 10 minutes before serving.

MAKE AHEAD The lasagna can be assembled but not baked, covered, and refrigerated up to 24 hours ahead. Bring to room temperature before baking. You may need to increase cooking time by about 5 minutes.

Seafood Lasagna

SERVES 8 TO 10

This recipe is surprisingly easy, especially if you use previously cooked and shelled shrimp. I've served it for Christmas Eve dinner to rave reviews—Mom especially loved it.

2 tablespoons butter

1 cup chopped yellow onion

8 ounces cream cheese at room temperature, cut into 8 squares

1½ cups ricotta cheese

1 egg, beaten

2 tablespoons chopped fresh basil, or 2 teaspoons dried

½ teaspoon salt

⅛ teaspoon ground pepper

2 cans (10 ounce) cream of mushroom soup

⅓ cup white wine or dry vermouth

5 ounces fresh lump crabmeat

1 pound medium shrimp, shelled, deveined and cooked

8 no-boil lasagna noodles

¼ cup grated Parmesan cheese

½ cup shredded sharp Cheddar cheese

Preheat oven to 350 degrees.

Melt the butter in a medium skillet over medium heat. Add the onion and cook until soft. Reduce heat to low, add cream cheese and ricotta and continue to cook, stirring until cheeses melt and are well combined. Remove from heat and stir in the egg, basil, salt and pepper. Set aside.

In a large mixing bowl, combine the soup and wine (or vermouth). Stir in the crab and shrimp.

Place 4 lasagna noodles in a 9x13-inch baking dish. Spread half the ricotta cheese mixture evenly over the noodles. Spread half the shrimp and crab mixture over the cheese layer. Place the remaining 4 lasagna noodles over the top and repeat the layers. Sprinkle the top with Parmesan and Cheddar cheeses. Bake, uncovered, for 45 minutes or until bubbly hot. Let stand 15 minutes before serving.

MAKE AHEAD The casserole can be made ahead, covered, and refrigerated up to 24 hours ahead. Can also be frozen. Bring to room temperature before baking.

172 **A WELL-SEASONED KITCHEN**

Chicken and Mushroom Lasagna with Tomato Sauce

SERVES 8 TO 10

Don't be intimidated by the length of this recipe—it has a lot of ingredients but doesn't take too much time to make, especially since so much can be done ahead.

TOMATO SAUCE

⅓ cup extra virgin olive oil
1 small carrot, chopped
½ small red onion, chopped
1 small leek, sliced
1 can (28 ounce) plum tomatoes (chopped), undrained
½ teaspoon chopped garlic
¾ cup chicken broth
½ cup dry white wine
⅛ teaspoon crushed red pepper
1 bay leaf
1 cup unsalted butter, cold and cut into small pieces
1 cup chopped Italian parsley
¾ teaspoon salt
½ teaspoon ground black pepper

LASAGNA

1¼ cups dried porcini mushrooms (1.5 ounces)
⅓ cup extra virgin olive oil
4 ounces mixed fresh, sliced mushrooms (button, shiitake or oyster)
1 teaspoon chopped garlic
¾ pound fresh spinach, stems removed and coarsely chopped
½ teaspoon dried oregano
1 teaspoon salt
½ teaspoon pepper
4½ cups chopped cooked chicken
1 pound mozzarella cheese, cut into ¼-inch cubes
2 cups ricotta cheese
1⅓ cups grated Pecorino Romano cheese
½ cup chopped fresh basil
No-boil lasagna noodles (enough for one lasagna)
½ cup shredded mozzarella cheese

First, make the tomato sauce: Heat the olive oil in a large saucepan over medium-high heat. Add the carrot, onion and leek and cook until soft, about 5 minutes. Add the tomatoes, juice and the garlic and continue cooking for another 5 minutes. Add chicken broth, white wine, red pepper and bay leaf. Increase heat to high and cook until the sauce is thick, about 20 to 25 minutes. Put the mixture in a food processor and puree until smooth. Set aside.

Preheat oven to 350 degrees. Lightly oil the bottom of a 9x13x2-inch baking dish.

In a small bowl, soak the dried porcini mushrooms in hot water until softened, about 20 minutes. Drain and rinse; pat dry and coarsely chop. Set aside.

In a large skillet or sauté pan, heat olive oil over medium-high heat. Add the sliced mushrooms and garlic and cook, stirring, until the mushrooms are softened, about 5 minutes. Add the chopped porcini mushrooms and cook another 2 minutes. Add the spinach, reduce the heat to medium and cook, stirring, until almost all of the liquid has evaporated and the spinach is cooked, about 10 minutes. Remove from the heat and stir in the oregano, salt, pepper and chopped chicken. Season with additional salt and pepper as needed. Set aside.

In a large mixing bowl, combine the mozzarella cubes, ricotta, Romano and basil. Line the bottom of the prepared baking dish with lasagna noodles to cover. Spread evenly with half of the cheese mixture. Cover with another layer of lasagna noodles. Spread all of the chicken–spinach mixture over the pasta. Season with salt and pepper. Cover with another layer of lasagna noodles, spread the remaining cheese mixture on top and cover with a final layer of noodles. Sprinkle the shredded mozzarella on top. Bake for 30 minutes or just until heated through—do not let it come to a boil! Preheat broiler and broil lasagna 4 inches from heat until top is brown. Cool for 10 minutes before serving.

While the lasagna is cooking, reheat the tomato sauce and whisk in the butter pieces. Stir in the chopped parsley, salt and pepper. Serve the sauce on the side (or pour some on top if plating the lasagna to serve).

MAKE AHEAD Tomato sauce can be made up to 24 hours ahead, covered and refrigerated. Lasagna can also be assembled but not baked up to 24 hours ahead, covered and refrigerated. Bring lasagna to room temperature before baking.

A well-seasoned memory

To keep things simple, Mom's dinner parties were often served buffet-style. At the end of cocktail hour, Mom would instruct everyone in the living room to proceed into the dining room to go through the line. Perhaps we'd done this so often that one evening, as the guests were gathering, my brother's golden retriever Frodo joined the buffet line with his dish in his mouth. If Mom's dinner parties weren't already legendary by then, this story cemented her place in dinner party lore!

Frodo getting in line for dinner!

vegetarian main dishes

Butternut Squash Gratin **page 178**

When I was living in Amsterdam, I learned how versatile, delicious and satisfying vegetarian main dishes can be. As a result, I've collected a number of recipes throughout the years that both my vegetarian friends and I enjoy. From the Butternut Squash Gratin to the Fondue, you'll be sure to find a vegetarian dish that hits the spot.

Butternut Squash Gratin

SERVES 4

I've been making this recipe for years and especially love preparing it for a fall evening when the air turns crisp and cool. Serve with mixed baby greens tossed with our Sharp Vinaigrette dressing. *(Photo, page 176)*

3 pounds butternut squash
1 teaspoon extra virgin olive oil
½ cup chopped leek
½ cup dry white wine
½ cup chicken broth
1 can (12 ounce) evaporated skim
  milk
½ teaspoon sugar
1 small French baguette
  (or half of a large)
1 cup shredded Gruyère cheese
  (4 ounces)
2 tablespoons grated Parmesan
  cheese

Preheat oven to 400 degrees. Butter a 6- to 8-cup shallow baking dish.

Cut the squash in half, remove the seeds and place, cut side up, in a rimmed baking pan. Season with salt and pepper, cover with aluminum foil and bake until tender but not mushy, around 1 hour. Set aside and let cool enough to handle. Leave the oven on.

While the squash is cooking, slice the baguette into 1/2-inch pieces and toast the slices until light brown. Set aside.

Heat the olive oil in a medium saucepan over medium heat. Add the chopped leek and 2 teaspoons water; cover and cook over medium-low heat until the leek is soft, about 5 minutes. Stir in the wine. Increase the heat to medium-high and boil, uncovered, for 3 minutes. Remove from the heat and stir in the chicken broth, milk and sugar. Add salt and pepper to taste. Once the squash is cool enough to handle, reheat the leek mixture.

Scoop the flesh from 1/2 of the squash into large pieces and place in the prepared baking dish, covering the bottom. Place approximately 1/2 of the baguette slices over the squash, to cover with space in between the slices. Cover with 1/2 of the leek mixture and 1/2 of the Gruyère cheese. Repeat layers. Sprinkle the top with the Parmesan cheese. Bake for 30 minutes, or until the top is brown and bubbly. Serve immediately.

MAKE AHEAD Gratin can be assembled but not baked earlier in the day, covered and refrigerated. Bring to room temperature before cooking.

Parmesan Polenta with Mushroom Marinara

SERVES 4

This recipe offers a wonderful, easy way to serve polenta. Once the cooked polenta comes out of the microwave, don't let it stand before serving as it will quickly harden.

MARINARA SAUCE

¼ cup extra virgin olive oil

8 ounces sliced fresh mushrooms

2 jars (14 ounce) prepared
   marinara sauce

1 cup dry red wine

¼ teaspoon red pepper flakes

½ cup chopped fresh Italian parsley

PARMESAN POLENTA

1¼ cups cornmeal

½ teaspoon salt

1 cup grated mozzarella cheese

1 cup grated Parmesan cheese,
   plus more for garnish

Heat olive oil in medium skillet over medium-high heat. Add mushrooms and sauté for about 5 minutes, until softened. Add marinara sauce, red wine and red pepper flakes. Simmer for about 15 minutes. Mix in parsley and season to taste with salt and pepper.

While the sauce is simmering, in a microwave-safe bowl, whisk together 4 cups of water, cornmeal and salt until blended. Cover and microwave on high for 5 minutes. Whisk until smooth. Re-cover and cook another 3 minutes. Let stand for 1 minute, then whisk in cheeses. Season to taste with salt and pepper.

Immediately divide polenta among four individual serving plates and top with sauce. Sprinkle with additional Parmesan cheese to taste. Serve immediately.

MAKE AHEAD Sauce can be made up to 3 days ahead, covered and refrigerated.

Roasted Eggplant, Zucchini and Red Pepper

SERVES 4

●

One night in Amsterdam, two of my dinner guests were vegetarian. I created this recipe especially for them—and they loved it. I've found this dish to be very flexible. You can use different types of cheese and add or subtract different roasted vegetables as you like.

8 slices eggplant
   (around ½ inch thick)
12 slices (rounds) zucchini
   (around ½ inch thick)
2 sweet red peppers, cored,
   seeded, each cut into 2 pieces
¼ cup extra virgin olive oil
½ cup prepared pesto, divided
2 cups Fontina cheese, divided

Preheat oven to 425 degrees. Grease a large baking sheet. Grease an 8x8-inch (or other shallow 2-quart) baking dish.

Brush both sides of the eggplant, zucchini and red pepper slices with olive oil and place in a single layer on the prepared baking sheet. Season with salt (preferably kosher) and pepper to taste. Bake for around 10 to 15 minutes or until soft and lightly brown. Reduce oven temperature to 375 degrees.

Place 4 slices of the roasted eggplant in the bottom of the prepared baking dish in one layer. Spread top with 1/4 cup pesto. Top with roasted red pepper slices. Top with roasted zucchini, then sprinkle with 1 cup of cheese. Place remaining 4 slices of roasted eggplant on top of the cheese. Spread remaining pesto, then remaining cheese on the top. Bake for around 15 to 20 minutes or until hot and the cheese has melted.

MAKE AHEAD Casserole can be assembled but not baked up to 24 hours in advance, covered and refrigerated. Bring to room temperature before baking.

VARIATION For a pretty presentation, bake in large individual ramekins. Cool slightly, run a knife around the edge and unmold.

Chile Relleno Casserole

SERVES 8 TO 10

●

This version of chile rellenos was always Mom's favorite ands she made it often—so often that family friend Reed Schroeder specifically asked for the recipe to be included in this book.

5 cans (4 ounce) whole green
  chiles
¾ pound grated sharp Cheddar
  cheese
¾ pound grated Monterey Jack
  cheese
4 eggs, separated
1 can (12 ounce) evaporated milk
2 tablespoons flour
1 can (15 ounce) tomato sauce

Preheat oven to 350 degrees. Grease a 9x13-inch baking dish.

Split chiles lengthwise on one side. Remove seeds, rinse and drain. Cover the bottom of the prepared casserole dish with half of the green chiles. Sprinkle the Cheddar evenly over the top. Spread the remaining chiles evenly over the cheese. Sprinkle the Monterey Jack cheese evenly over the top. Set aside.

With an electric mixer, beat the egg yolks until smooth. Add the milk, flour and salt and pepper to taste and continue beating until well mixed. In another bowl, with an electric mixer beat the egg whites until stiff. Stir 1/4 of the beaten egg whites into the egg yolk mixture; gently fold in the rest of the egg whites just until mixed. Pour evenly over the top of the cheese in the baking dish. Bake for 45 minutes or until set. Remove from the oven and pour the tomato sauce evenly over the top. Place back in the oven just until the sauce on top is heated through, around 10 to 15 minutes. Let sit for a few minutes before serving.

MAKE AHEAD The casserole can be assembled and baked through putting the tomato sauce on the top, covered and refrigerated for up to 1 day. Reheat at 350 degrees for at least 30 minutes.

Pesto and Ricotta Cheese Soufflé

SERVES 4

●

Perfect for a casual Sunday night supper.

6 eggs, separated
2 tablespoons flour
½ teaspoon salt
Freshly ground black pepper
   to taste
⅓ cup freshly grated Parmesan
   cheese (plus more to coat
   the dish)
1 cup prepared pesto
2 cups ricotta cheese

Preheat oven to 375 degrees. Butter a 2-quart soufflé dish and sprinkle it with grated Parmesan cheese.

In a large mixing bowl, whisk together the egg yolks, flour, salt, pepper, 1/3 cup Parmesan cheese and pesto. Add the ricotta cheese and whisk until well combined.

Beat the egg whites with an electric mixer until they form stiff peaks. Stir 1/4 of the egg whites into the ricotta cheese mixture; gently fold in remaining egg whites. Transfer to the prepared soufflé dish. Place in the oven and immediately reduce the temperature to 350 degrees. Bake undisturbed for 45 minutes. Serve immediately.

Mushroom, Tomato and Cream Cheese Enchiladas

SERVES 6 TO 8

●

A dish so delicious your carnivore friends won't even notice the lack of meat!

TOMATO SAUCE
1 tablespoon extra virgin olive oil
½ cup chopped yellow onion
½ teaspoon chopped garlic
1 can (28 ounce) diced tomatoes, undrained
1 tablespoon honey
3 teaspoons chili powder, divided
½ teaspoon ground cumin
½ teaspoon ground coriander
Dash cayenne pepper

ENCHILADA FILLING
2 tablespoons butter
12 ounces fresh mushrooms, sliced
8 ounces cream cheese, cut up
1 cup sour cream
¾ cup sliced green onions
8 7-inch flour tortillas
1 can (2¼ ounce) sliced black olives, drained
¾ cup grated Monterey Jack or Pepper Jack cheese

Preheat oven to 350 degrees. Grease a 9x13-inch baking dish.

To make the tomato sauce, heat the olive oil in a large saucepan over medium heat. When hot, add the onion and garlic and cook until onion is tender. Stir in the diced tomatoes, honey, 1 teaspoon of the chili powder, cumin, coriander and cayenne pepper. Bring to a boil, reduce heat and simmer, uncovered, for around 30 minutes, stirring occasionally. Season to taste with salt and pepper. Set aside.

To make the filling, melt the butter in a large saucepan over medium heat and sauté the mushrooms with the remaining 2 teaspoons of chili powder for about 10 minutes, until the mushrooms are tender and liquid is cooked off. Reduce the heat to low, stir in the cream cheese until melted, then stir in the sour cream and green onions. Season to taste with salt and pepper.

Spread 1/4 cup of the tomato sauce evenly over the bottom of the prepared dish. Dip 1 side of 1 tortilla in the remaining tomato mixture. Spoon 1/3 cup of the mushroom mixture onto the center of the dry side of the tortilla. Sprinkle with 1/8 of the sliced olives. Roll up and place, seam side down, in the prepared baking dish. Repeat with remaining 7 tortillas. Spoon remaining tomato sauce over the tortillas, covering completely. Cover and bake in the top third of the oven for around 30 minutes or until heated through. Uncover, sprinkle the grated Jack cheese over the top and continue baking, uncovered, just until cheese melts, around 4 to 5 minutes. Serve immediately.

MAKE AHEAD Enchiladas can be assembled but not baked earlier in the day, covered, and refrigerated. Bring to room temperature before baking. Tomato sauce can be made up to 3 days ahead, covered and refrigerated.

Tex-Mex Cheese Fondue

SERVES 6

●

A slight modification of the basic ingredients in cheese fondue results in a delicious and different south-of-the-border flavor. This is a fun fondue to serve for a casual gathering in the mountains *après ski*.

1¼ pounds shredded Gruyère cheese
1 pound shredded Monterey Jack cheese
¼ cup flour
1 clove garlic
2½ cups dry white wine
3 tablespoons tequila
¼ cup chopped fresh cilantro (or more to taste)
2 tablespoons chopped fresh jalapeño pepper (include seeds for more heat)

French bread cubes
Broccoli and/or cauliflower heads
Carrots, sliced 1 inch thick
Sliced cooked sausage, such as chorizo (for the non-vegetarians in the crowd)

Place both cheeses in a large mixing bowl, add the flour and toss to coat. Set aside.

Rub the inside of a fondue pot with the garlic. Add the wine and tequila and heat over medium heat until the mixture is almost boiling. Add a handful of cheese and stir constantly until the cheese melts, reducing heat slightly if the mixture starts to boil. Keep stirring and adding handfuls of cheese until the mixture is thick and creamy. Stir in the cilantro and jalapeños. Season to taste with salt and pepper.

Set pot over sterno in the middle of the table. Pass the bread cubes, vegetables and sausage for dipping.

side dishes

Kentucky Corn Pudding **page 198**

Selecting the right side dish can make all the difference in a meal in terms of both taste and presentation. I can still hear Mom say "always include one green vegetable and one starch!" I like to also include some other colors on a plate, especially when serving a main dish with limited color.

Stuffed Tomatoes Provençal with Parsley, Pine Nuts and Wine

SERVES 6

We love serving tomatoes as a side dish with steak or other beef at a dinner party. The flavors are perfectly matched, and the tomatoes add color to the plate.

6 medium vine-ripened tomatoes
1 cup chopped fresh parsley
½ cup pine nuts
½ teaspoon seasoned salt
    (Lowry's or Jane's)
2 teaspoons minced garlic
2 tablespoons fresh lemon juice
    (approximately ½ lemon)
3 tablespoons olive oil
2 tablespoons dry white wine

Preheat oven to 350 degrees. Oil a baking dish large enough to hold 12 tomato halves.

Halve the tomatoes and remove the seeds with a small spoon (I like to use a grapefruit spoon). Place the tomatoes, cut side up, in the prepared baking dish. Combine the parsley, pine nuts, salt, garlic, lemon juice, olive oil and white wine. Fill the hollow tomato cavities with the nut mixture. Sprinkle top with seasoned salt and fresh ground pepper. Bake for 15 to 20 minutes or until heated through.

MAKE AHEAD Tomatoes can be stuffed earlier in the day, covered and kept at room temperature. Bake before serving.

Cauliflower Purée

This simple dish is delicious with a texture and taste very similar to mashed potatoes—and much faster and easier to make. If you prefer to omit the garlic, the purée tastes equally good without it.

1 head cauliflower
3 tablespoons butter or margarine
2 tablespoons cream cheese
½ to ¾ teaspoon chopped garlic
(optional)

Cut the cauliflower into florets, discarding base and leaves. Cut the larger florets in two. Place florets in a steamer rack over boiling water, cover and steam until very tender (around 12 to 15 minutes, depending on how small you cut the florets). While hot, place cooked florets in a food processor with the remaining ingredients. Blend until puréed and smooth. Season with salt and pepper (takes a fair amount of salt). Serve immediately.

MAKE AHEAD Purée can be made up to 24 hours ahead, covered and refrigerated. Reheat in a saucepan over low heat; can also be reheated in a microwave.

Creamed Spinach and Tomato Gratin

SERVES 6

Scrumptious and pretty, too! If you prefer to omit the tomato and bread crumb topping, you can simply heat the spinach mixture on the stove—it's just as delicious.

1 tablespoon butter

½ small yellow onion, chopped

2 green onions, chopped

½ cup chicken broth

½ cup heavy cream

¼ to ½ teaspoon salt
(depends on amount of sodium in the chicken broth you use)

½ teaspoon ground black pepper

⅛ teaspoon ground nutmeg

2 packages (10 ounce) frozen chopped spinach, thawed and squeezed dry

6 slices tomato (¼-inch thick)

¼ cup bread crumbs

4 tablespoons grated Parmesan cheese

Preheat oven to 375 degrees. Spray a 1-quart gratin or shallow baking dish with cooking spray.

In a medium skillet, melt butter over medium heat. Cook yellow and green onions until softened, about 5 to 7 minutes. Stir in broth, cream, salt, pepper and nutmeg. Bring to a boil, reduce heat to medium and cook 15 minutes, until liquid is reduced to 2/3 cup and coats the back of a spoon. Stir in spinach. Spoon into prepared dish and top with tomato slices. Mix together bread crumbs and Parmesan cheese and sprinkle over the top of the tomatoes. Bake for 20 to 30 minutes or until golden brown on top.

MAKE AHEAD Gratin can be prepared but not baked earlier in the day, covered and refrigerated. Bring to room temperature before cooking.

Green Beans with Cashew Gremolata

SERVES 4

●

Traditionally, a gremolata contains chopped garlic, parsley and lemon zest. Cooks today mix and match different ingredients to enhance various dishes. In this recipe, we substitute chopped cashews, pecans, or pine nuts for the garlic, and the flavors work well with the green beans.

¼ cup roasted cashew pieces (salted okay) – can substitute toasted pine nuts or toasted chopped pecans
2 tablespoons chopped parsley
1½ teaspoons lemon zest
2 tablespoons extra virgin olive oil
½ pound fresh green beans

In a small mixing bowl, stir together the nuts, parsley, lemon zest and olive oil. Set aside. Trim green beans, cut into 1- to 1 1/2-inch pieces and steam until crisp-tender, about 8 minutes. Place cooked beans in a serving bowl and toss with nut mixture. Season to taste with salt and pepper. Serve immediately.

Green Beans with Lemon-Butter Sauce

SERVES 4

So easy, yet so delicious...

2 tablespoons unsalted butter
1 teaspoon grated lemon zest
2 teaspoons fresh lemon juice
¼ teaspoon salt
¼ teaspoon freshly ground black
    pepper
4 cups green beans, trimmed

Melt butter in the microwave or on the stove top. Stir in lemon zest, lemon juice, salt and pepper. In a separate pot, steam green beans until crisp-tender. Place in a serving bowl and toss with lemon-butter sauce. Season to taste with additional salt and pepper and serve immediately.

A well-seasoned memory

Some cooking adventures result in big lessons learned! One year, I was cooking Individual Asparagus Soufflés for a birthday celebration. Family friend Greg Stanbro kept me company in the kitchen while I cooked. He watched me load all the soufflé ingredients into the food processor and hit the start button. He and I watched in horror as green sauce exploded out of the processor onto the counter and all over the floor. Greg immediately asked, "What can I do?" to which I instinctively replied "Get my Mom!" First lesson learned: always put the ingredients into the food processor in batches when doubling a recipe. Second lesson learned: when in doubt about how to rescue a dinner—call Mom!

Sally and Mack at her 75th birthday party.

Individual Asparagus Soufflés

SERVES 6

These are incredibly easy to make—no beating or folding of egg whites. Everything goes into the food processor, and presto! you have six soufflés. If you double this recipe, process it in two batches unless you have a very large food processor. I tried to do it all at once and ended up with soufflé batter all over my kitchen!

6 teaspoons Parmesan cheese
1 pound fresh asparagus, trimmed
7 large eggs
⅓ cup heavy cream
½ cup shredded Gruyère cheese
1 teaspoon Dijon mustard
½ teaspoon salt
¼ teaspoon ground pepper
⅛ teaspoon ground nutmeg
8 ounces ricotta cheese

Preheat oven to 375 degrees. Butter six 6-ounce ramekins or soufflé dishes. Sprinkle 1 teaspoon of Parmesan cheese into each dish and roll it around to coat the sides and bottom with cheese. Place on a rimmed cookie sheet.

Cut the asparagus into 1 to 1 1/2-inch pieces and steam until just tender, 5 to 7 minutes. Set aside to cool.

In a food processor, combine the eggs, cream, Gruyère cheese, mustard, salt, pepper and nutmeg. Blend until smooth. With the machine running, add the asparagus pieces a few at a time. Gradually add the ricotta cheese in spoonfuls and continue processing until smooth. Pour into prepared dishes.

Bake for 20 to 25 minutes or until a toothpick inserted in the center comes out clean. Serve immediately.

Kentucky Corn Pudding

SERVES 6

This was one of Mom's signature dishes. The recipe came from her mother, Nama, and was passed to all of her grandchildren. It is a traditional Kentucky dish that even Yankees love—just ask our friend Cynthia who lives in Boston and serves it often at dinner parties! *(Photo, page 188)*

3 eggs
2 cups corn (4 ears fresh or 2
   packages frozen, thawed slightly)
2 tablespoons sugar
1 teaspoon salt
2 tablespoons flour
2 cups whole milk
2 tablespoons butter, melted

Preheat oven to 350 degrees.

Place eggs, corn, sugar, salt and flour in a blender and blend until barely blended (you should have some whole corn kernels). Pour into a 7x11-inch glass baking dish. Heat milk over high heat until slightly scalded and add to casserole, mixing well. Pour melted butter over the top (do not stir). Place casserole dish in a larger glass dish that is half full of hot water. Bake for 1 to 1 1/2 hours, stirring from the bottom 2 to 3 times during baking.

NOTE If pudding gets watery at the end, leave in the oven for a few more minutes. Take out and let sit for a few minutes, stir, then let it sit a minute or two more. Most of the excess water should be absorbed.

Leek Gratin

SERVES 8 TO 10

This recipe is excellent as part of a Thanksgiving menu—an updated version of the traditional creamed onion dish.

8 hard boiled eggs, peeled
10 medium leeks
6 tablespoons butter, divided
2 tablespoons flour
1½ cups whole milk
½ cup shredded white Cheddar cheese (around 2 ounces), divided
¼ cup grated Parmesan cheese
¼ teaspoon cayenne pepper

Preheat oven to 450 degrees.

Cut each hard-boiled egg into 8 pieces. Arrange in a single layer in a 1 1/2- to 2-quart gratin dish (or a 10-inch pie pan). Set aside.

Remove and discard dark green portion of leeks. Cut off the root end and cut each leek in half lengthwise. Rinse well, making sure to remove all the dirt. Pat dry. Coarsely chop leeks. In a large skillet, melt 4 tablespoons of the butter over medium heat. Add the leeks and cook until tender, about 5 to 7 minutes. Spoon the cooked leeks over the top of the eggs in the gratin dish—don't wash the skillet.

In the same skillet, melt the remaining 2 tablespoons of butter over low heat. Whisk in the flour and cook for 3 minutes, whisking constantly. Slowly begin to whisk in the milk, increase the heat to medium and cook sauce, whisking, until bubbly and thickened. Whisk in 1/4 cup of the Cheddar, the Parmesan and cayenne pepper. Season to taste with salt and pepper. Pour sauce evenly over the leeks and eggs; sprinkle top with remaining 1/4 cup Cheddar. Bake for 10 minutes or until bubbly and top is golden brown.

MAKE AHEAD Gratin can be assembled but not baked earlier in the day, covered and stored in the refrigerator. Bring to room temperature before baking.

Sausage, Butternut Squash and Yam Casserole

SERVES 8

This recipe has become a Clayton family Thanksgiving tradition, and has been adopted by many other homes that I have taken it to as part of a potluck dinner. We don't like yam dishes that are too sweet and haven't been able to find another recipe we like as much as this one. Another bonus? You can make it ahead and freeze it, reducing holiday stress.

1¾ pounds yams, peeled and chopped

1¾ pounds butternut squash, peeled, seeded and chopped

2 tablespoons butter, melted

¼ teaspoon ground nutmeg

1 pound bulk pork sausage

½ cup chopped green onions, (or more to taste)

1 cup grated sharp Cheddar cheese

¼ cup finely chopped pecans

Preheat oven to 350 degrees. Butter a 2- or 3-quart shallow baking or gratin dish.

Steam the yams and squash until tender enough to mash, about 20 minutes. Remove from the heat and transfer to a mixing bowl. Mash into large chunks, add the butter and nutmeg. Season generously with salt and pepper.

Cook the sausage in a skillet over medium heat, stirring and breaking up. After 5 minutes (when the sausage is about half browned), add the green onions and sauté until the sausage is cooked through, stirring occasionally and continuing to break up into bits, about 10 more minutes. Remove from the heat, strain off the fat and set aside.

Spread half the yam/squash mixture in the prepared baking dish, top with half the sausage and half the grated cheese. Repeat the layers, and top with chopped nuts.

Bake for 30 minutes or until heated through and the cheese is bubbly and the top is brown.

MAKE AHEAD The casserole can be prepared earlier in the day, covered and refrigerated, or frozen for up to a month. Return to room temperature before baking.

Grilled Vegetable Packets

SERVES 6

In our household, my husband does the dishes! And, he's not happy when I make dinner using all the pots and pans we have. Pairing this recipe with a grilled main dish means few, if any, pots for him to wash—oh, and he loves the recipe, too!

1 medium zucchini, cut into
   1-inch cubes
1 medium yellow squash,
   cut into 1-inch cubes
½ pound eggplant, cut into
   1-inch cubes
6 small red potatoes, cut into
   ½-inch cubes
1 medium red onion, sliced
2 tablespoons olive oil
½ cup crumbled tomato and basil
   flavored goat cheese or
   flavored feta
2 teaspoons chopped garlic
1 tablespoon chopped fresh basil

Preheat grill.

In a large mixing bowl, toss all the ingredients until mixed. Season with salt and pepper.

Spray 6 large sheets of foil (12x15 inches) with cooking spray. Divide the vegetables among the sheets. Fold up sides to create a pouch, leaving a place at the top for the steam to escape.

Turn the grill to medium (or let coals cool to medium temperature), place packets on grill rack. Grill, cover closed, for 30 to 35 minutes or until the vegetables are crisp tender.

VARIATION You can use almost any mixture of vegetables and onions for this dish.

Veggie Fries with Lemon-Garlic Aioli

SERVES 4 TO 6

This is a wonderful alternative to French fries. In addition to serving these fries as a side dish, I have also served these as an appetizer at a cocktail party. Let the aioli sit for about an hour before serving—it gives the flavors a chance to blend. Any leftover aioli is great on sandwiches, too.

GARLIC AIOLI
1 cup mayonnaise
¼ cup chopped fresh parsley
2 teaspoons chopped fresh garlic
2 tablespoons fresh lemon juice

FRIES
¼ cup flour
1 egg
½ cup Italian bread crumbs
⅓ cup grated Parmesan cheese
4 large Portobello mushrooms
2 medium zucchini
Vegetable oil for frying

In small mixing bowl, whisk together the mayonnaise, parsley, garlic and lemon juice to make the aioli. Cover and refrigerate until ready to use.

Place the flour in a shallow dish. In another shallow dish, whisk together the egg and 1 tablespoon of water. In a third shallow dish, stir together the bread crumbs and Parmesan cheese. Set aside.

Stem the mushrooms and scrape out the dark gills on the inside (I like to use a grapefruit spoon). Cut off the rough edges around the rim. Slice into 1/2-inch wedges. Slice off the ends of the zucchini, cut in half horizontally, and cut each half into 1/2-inch wedges. Toss the mushroom and zucchini wedges in the flour to coat evenly, shaking off excess. Coat in egg mixture then roll in bread crumb mixture to coat. In a large frying pan, pour oil to depth of around 1 inch and heat over medium-high heat. Fry veggie fries until dark golden brown. Drain on paper towels and serve with the garlic aioli on the side.

MAKE AHEAD The veggies can be breaded, covered and refrigerated for up to 2 hours before frying. Once fried, they can be held, in a dish lined with paper towel, in a warming oven or very low temperature oven for up to 1 hour.

Everyone in our family loves the flavor of roasted vegetables—and also the ease and speed of cooking. You can use this recipe for just about any vegetable—or combination of vegetables. A few examples are provided, but use your imagination!

Extra virgin olive oil (good quality)
Kosher salt
Vegetable(s) of choice

Preheat the oven to 425 degrees.

Clean vegetables—peel and/or chop as needed per directions below. Sprinkle liberally with olive oil and kosher salt and toss (we like to use our hands), adding any additional seasonings noted. Roast in oven, stirring halfway through, for recommended time. Toss with recommended seasoning and serve.

VEGGIE SUGGESTIONS

VEGETABLE	PREPARATION	TIMING	SEASONING (POST-ROASTING)
Asparagus	Break off tough ends	10 minutes	Fresh ground pepper Parmesan cheese (optional)
Cauliflower	Cut into florets	15 minutes	Parmesan cheese and mixed herbs Or, curry powder mixed with olive oil and lemon juice
Green beans	break off ends	10 minutes	Parmesan cheese and lemon zest
Turnips	Peel and cut into 2x1/2-inch sticks and sprinkle with 1/2 teaspoon chili powder	30 minutes	Nothing more is needed
Winter squash (Can use butternut, hubbard, acorn, etc.)	Peel, seed and cut into 1/2-inch square pieces; add chopped Italian parsley, chopped garlic	30 minutes	Fresh ground pepper

Roasted New Potatoes with Truffle Oil

SERVES 6

I was first introduced to this style of potatoes when I was in the Umbrian region of Italy vacationing with our close friend Don Greco. I love truffle oil and it tastes delicious with potatoes, either roasted or fried. Be careful never to add truffle oil when baking as the cooking process will remove the truffle flavor.

2 pounds (about 16 potatoes) medium red-skinned new potatoes, cut into eighths (or quarters if small)

3 tablespoons extra virgin olive oil

Kosher salt

2 tablespoons chopped Italian parsley

¼ cup grated Parmesan cheese

2 tablespoons white truffle oil or more to taste (careful, it has a strong flavor!)

Preheat oven to 425 degrees. Spray a 9x13-inch baking dish with nonstick cooking spray.

Place potatoes in the prepared baking dish and toss with olive oil and kosher salt (to taste). Bake, stirring occasionally, for 35 to 40 minutes or until potatoes are tender when poked with a fork. Remove from oven and toss with chopped parsley, Parmesan cheese and truffle oil.

NOTE These can be baked at 375 degrees on the lower rack in the oven, which means that you can cook them together with other dishes if needed. Just increase the baking time to 45 to 55 minutes.

Overnight Potato Salad

SERVES 8

Potato salad is one of my all-time favorites. As the name indicates, you need to start making this salad the day before serving.

3 eggs
5 medium Idaho potatoes
1 slice yellow onion
5 to 6 peppercorns
⅛ cup olive oil
⅛ cup white wine vinegar
1 tablespoon Dijon mustard
2 to 3 green onions, chopped
2 ribs celery, sliced
1 cucumber, peeled, seeded and chopped
2 teaspoons capers
⅓ cup mayonnaise (or more to taste)
Salt and pepper to taste

Hard boil the eggs, cool, then peel and chop. Place in a bowl and refrigerate.

Place the whole unpeeled potatoes, onion slice and peppercorns in a large saucepan. Cover with salted water, bring to a boil and cook until just fork-tender. Do not overcook or your salad will be mushy! Drain the water from the pan, take out the onion slice and peppercorns, and return the pan with the potatoes to the heat. Shake the potatoes over medium heat constantly until dry, about 1 minute. Let cool until you are able to handle, then peel and cut into bite-size chunks and place in a large bowl. Season with salt and pepper.

In a small bowl, whisk together the olive oil, vinegar and mustard and carefully toss the potatoes with the dressing, making sure not to mash them. Place potatoes in the refrigerator, uncovered, overnight.

Take the potatoes out of the refrigerator and add the chopped eggs, green onion, celery, cucumbers and capers and carefully mix. Add enough mayonnaise to moisten the salad and toss well. Refrigerate until serving time. Season to taste with salt and pepper.

NOTE If you are pressed for time, you can refrigerate the potatoes for about 4 hours—but it tastes best if you let the flavors combine overnight.

Potato Soufflé

SERVES 4

Mom has had this recipe for years and served it both for family meals and at several dinner parties. My brother Jim and I loved these as kids—who wouldn't with all this cheese?

3 small Idaho potatoes
1 egg
1 cup ricotta cheese
½ cup half and half
1 cup grated Gruyère cheese, divided
1½ teaspoons salt

Preheat oven to 350 degrees. Grease an 8x8-inch baking dish.

Peel the potatoes and cut into 1/2- to 1-inch cubes. Place in a medium saucepan and cover with water. Bring to a boil, reduce the heat, cover and simmer until potatoes are tender, around 15 minutes. Drain and mash. Set aside.

While the potatoes are cooking, in a medium mixing bowl, whisk together the egg and ricotta cheese. Whisk in the half and half and 3/4 cup of the Gruyère cheese. Stir in the mashed potatoes. Season to taste with salt and pepper. Put in the prepared baking dish and bake until heated through and set, about 45 minutes. Sprinkle the remaining 1/4 cup Gruyère cheese over the top and continue baking until the cheese melts.

MAKE AHEAD The soufflé can be prepared but not baked earlier in the day, covered and refrigerated. Bring to room temperature before baking and increase cooking time to 1 hour.

Simone's Mayonnaise for French Fries

MAKES 1 CUP

Simone Geens is a Belgian friend who lived in Denver, with her husband Staf and children, for a year when I was growing up. They are still good friends of our family today. Simone is a gourmet cook, and one of the many delicious dishes she made for me when I visited them in Belgium was this wonderful mayonnaise, which she served with her homemade French fries.

1 egg
1 tablespoon Dijon mustard
1 cup corn oil
3 tablespoons tarragon white
  wine vinegar
Salt and pepper to taste

Put all ingredients in a fat, empty jam or Dijon mustard jar. Mix with an immersion blender until the consistency of mayonnaise.

Lemon Rice

A creamy rice dish that is great to serve in the spring or summer.

3 cups chicken broth
½ cup unsalted butter
2 cups long grain white rice
Zest of 2 lemons
1 teaspoon salt
2 tablespoons fresh lemon juice
1 cup heavy cream

Place the chicken broth in a medium saucepan and bring to a boil. Reduce heat to low.

In a separate large saucepan, melt the butter over low heat. Stir in rice and lemon zest. Cook over medium heat, stirring for 5 minutes. Stir in the hot broth and salt, cover and simmer for around 20 minutes or until liquid is absorbed. Stir in the lemon juice, then stir in the cream. Continue to stir over low heat until the cream is absorbed, around 5 minutes. Season with salt and pepper to taste.

LIGHTER VERSION Prepare as above, omitting the cream.

VARIATION Reduce cream to 1/2 cup, and when you add the cream, also add 1/4 cup grated Parmesan cheese and 1/4 cup chopped fresh parsley.

Brown Rice Gratin

SERVES 6

This recipe offers an easy and delicious way to enjoy the added nutrients found in brown rice.

3 cups cooked brown rice
¾ cup chicken broth
1 cup shredded Gruyère cheese
½ cup sour cream
⅔ cup chopped green onion
2 tablespoons Dijon mustard
¼ teaspoon fresh ground pepper
½ cup bread crumbs
4 teaspoon melted butter

Preheat oven to 350 degrees.

In a large mixing bowl, stir together the rice, broth, cheese, sour cream, green onion, mustard and pepper. Season to taste with salt. Spread evenly in a 9x13-inch casserole dish. Mix together the bread crumbs and melted butter and sprinkle over the top. Bake for around 15 to 20 minutes, until hot and crumbs are browned. If the gratin is hot but the crumbs are not brown after 20 minutes, switch the oven heat over to broil for a few minutes to brown the top.

VARIATION Add 2 cups cooked, coarsely chopped broccoli before topping with bread crumbs.

MAKE AHEAD Gratin can be assembled but not baked earlier in the day, covered and refrigerated. Bring to room temperature before baking.

Bobby Lewis' Wild Rice

Bobby Lewis is a great friend who, fortunately for all of us, was willing to share her delicious recipe for wild rice. This heavenly rice tastes great with any entrée, especially pork or chicken.

1 cup wild rice
3 cans (10 ounce) chicken broth
Zest from 1 orange
1 cup pecan halves
1 cup golden raisins
¼ cup chopped fresh mint
4 green onions, thinly sliced
¼ cup olive oil
⅓ cup fresh orange juice
1½ teaspoons salt

Rinse rice under running water. In a medium saucepan, combine rice and chicken broth. Cover and cook for around 45 minutes or until done. Drain and place in a large mixing bowl. Add remaining ingredients and toss gently. Let mixture stand for at least two hours. Season to taste with salt and pepper. Can be served at room temperature or warmed.

MAKE AHEAD Rice can be made 1 day ahead, covered and refrigerated.

Elegant Wild Rice Salad

SERVES 10 TO 12

This recipe is courtesy of my good friend Diane Heidel. She served this at my bridal shower, and Mom and I loved it so much we decided on the spot that it had to be included in our cookbook!

SALAD

3 cups wild rice, rinsed, or a mixture of wild with white and/or brown rice

2 jars (6 ounce) marinated artichoke hearts

1 package (10 ounce) frozen peas, thawed and drained

1 green bell pepper, chopped

1 bunch green onions, chopped

1 pint small cherry tomatoes, halved

Toasted slivered almonds

DRESSING

1⅓ cups vegetable oil

½ cup white wine vinegar

¼ cup grated Parmesan cheese

1 tablespoon sugar

2 teaspoons salt

1 teaspoon celery salt

½ teaspoon ground white pepper

½ teaspoon dry mustard

¼ teaspoon paprika

1 clove garlic, minced

½ marinade from artichoke hearts (from 1 jar)

In a large saucepan, heat 2 quarts and 1 cup water and rice to boiling. Reduce heat to low, cover and simmer for 45 minutes or until rice is done. Drain off any remaining liquid. Drain artichoke hearts, reserving marinade for dressing. Chop artichoke hearts and add to rice with thawed peas, green pepper, green onions, tomatoes and half of the reserved marinade. Set aside.

In a large lidded jar, combine all dressing ingredients and shake well. Toss half into rice mixture. Cover and chill. Just before serving, toss again and taste. Add additional dressing as needed and season to taste with salt and pepper. Sprinkle with slivered almonds and serve.

MAKE AHEAD Rice salad can be made the night before and refrigerated.

Vegetable Couscous with Dill Vinaigrette

SERVES 6

This dish can be made with any variation of the vegetable ingredients and it is still delicious.

COUSCOUS

1½ cups couscous
2¼ cups chicken broth
2 cups sliced fresh spinach
1 cup sliced mushrooms
½ cup frozen peas, thawed
   and drained
½ cup finely chopped jicama
¼ cup toasted pine nuts
3 to 4 green onions, chopped
2 ounces mozzarella cheese,
   chopped

VINAIGRETTE

⅓ cup extra virgin olive oil
¼ cup fresh lemon juice
1 tablespoon Dijon mustard
1 teaspoon lemon zest
⅛ teaspoon cumin
½ teaspoon chopped garlic
2 tablespoons chopped fresh dill

Place couscous in a large skillet and toast over medium heat until lightly browned. Add chicken broth and bring to a boil. Cover, remove from heat and let stand for at least 5 to 10 minutes, until the water is absorbed. Fluff couscous with a fork. Place couscous in a large mixing bowl with spinach, mushrooms, peas, jicama, pine nuts, onions and cheese. Stir to combine.

In a small bowl, whisk together the olive oil, lemon juice, mustard, lemon zest, cumin, garlic and dill. Pour over couscous mixture and toss to combine. Serve at room temperature.

MAKE AHEAD Couscous mixture and vinaigrette can be made earlier in the day and stored separately, covered, and in the refrigerator. If you plan to make it ahead, blend the vinaigrette ingredients together in a jar with a tight fitting lid—then all you need to do is give it a quick shake before tossing.

Creamy Parmesan Polenta

SERVES 6

This should really be called "To Die For Creamy Parmesan Polenta," it is so delicious. It goes well with virtually any meat or pork dish, especially our Fall-Off-the-Bone Slow Cooker Short Ribs.

2 cups chicken broth
2 cups heavy cream
  (or half and half)
1 cup yellow cornmeal
2 tablespoons unsalted butter
½ cup grated Parmesan cheese

Combine chicken broth and cream in a heavy saucepan and bring to a slow boil over medium-high heat. Slowly whisk in the cornmeal until completely incorporated. Reduce heat to medium-low and continue whisking until the mixture becomes thickened, around 10 to 12 minutes. Reduce heat to low, add the butter and Parmesan cheese and stir until both are melted. Add salt to taste (usually needs around 1/2 to 1 teaspoon). Serve immediately.

Cheese Grits

This recipe came from Nama, Mom's mother. Nama was a true Southern woman who loved her grits! (Mom made a few modifications to this recipe over the years).

4 cups whole milk
6 ounces Gruyère cheese, shredded
6 tablespoons butter
1 cup grits
1 teaspoon Jane's Krazy Mixed Up Salt
Cayenne pepper to taste
2 eggs, beaten
⅓ cup melted butter
⅓ cup Parmesan cheese

Preheat oven to 400 degrees. Butter a shallow casserole dish.

In a large stock pot, bring milk and Gruyère cheese to a boil. Stir in 6 tablespoons butter, grits, salt and cayenne pepper. Reduce heat to medium and cook until thick. Whisk in 2 eggs and cook, stirring constantly, for 5 minutes. Pour into prepared dish. Cover with 1/3 cup melted butter, then parmesan cheese—don't stir. Bake for 30 minutes.

Herb Quick Bread

MAKES 1 LOAF

A great bread to serve with soup or any of our main dish salads. I have also served it with meat dishes like Steaks with Dijon, Caper and Green Onion Sauce to rave reviews. It is incredibly easy to make and everyone loves it.

1 cup whole wheat flour
½ cup all purpose flour
½ cup cornmeal
2 teaspoons baking powder
½ teaspoon baking soda
½ teaspoon salt
1 teaspoon dried dill
½ teaspoon dried oregano
½ teaspoon dried basil
½ teaspoon dried thyme
¼ teaspoon fennel seeds
1¼ cups buttermilk
1 egg, beaten
2 tablespoons honey
2 tablespoons vegetable oil
1 tablespoon sesame seeds

Preheat oven to 350 degrees. Grease a 9x5-inch loaf pan.

In a large mixing bowl, whisk together the flours, cornmeal, baking powder, baking soda, salt, dill, oregano, basil, thyme and fennel. Set aside.

In a medium mixing bowl, whisk together the buttermilk, egg, honey and oil. Stir into the flour mixture just until blended. Spoon into the prepared loaf pan. Sprinkle top with sesame seeds. Bake for 40 to 45 minutes or until tester inserted in the middle comes out clean. Let cool in the pan for a few minutes, then turn out onto a wire rack to cool completely.

HIGH ALTITUDE No adjustments necessary.

MAKE AHEAD Bread can be made up to 2 days ahead, wrapped in foil and kept at room temperature.

Nama's Rolls

•

Mom's mother, Nama, was famous for her rolls. All of her children, and most of her grandchildren, know how to make them, as they are absolutely the best!

½ cup butter (or lard)
½ cup sugar
1 teaspoon salt
1 egg, beaten
1 envelope yeast
6 to 8 cups flour

With an electric mixer, cream together butter, sugar and salt. Beat in 1 cup boiling water and egg. Dissolve yeast in a small amount of warm water. Stir into mixture along with a second cup of (room temperature) water. Stir in 6 cups of flour. Add additional flour if dough is too sticky.

Flour work surface. Knead dough until smooth and elastic; about 5 to 8 minutes. Roll out to 1/2-inch thick and cut out rolls with 2 inch circle. Dip in butter and place side by side in a 9-inch cake pan or 7x11-inch baking dish. Alternatively, fold the circles in half to form an envelope shape and place in pan side by side. Let rise for 1 hour before baking. Bake at 350 degrees for around 20 minutes or until golden.

MAKE AHEAD The yeast dough can be made and rolls formed earlier in the day, covered and refrigerated until ready to use. Let rise for at least 1 hour, possibly more, before baking.

Parmesan-Buttermilk Cornbread

SERVES 6 TO 8

Mom loved cornbread, especially this recipe. The buttermilk and Parmesan cheese give this bread a nice tangy flavor.

1 cup flour
1 cup cornmeal (stone-ground)
¼ cup freshly grated Parmesan cheese
½ teaspoon baking soda
2 teaspoons baking powder
1 teaspoon salt
1 egg, beaten
1 cup buttermilk
¾ cup water
¼ cup vegetable oil
2 tablespoons chopped yellow onion

Preheat oven to 425 degrees. Grease a 7x11-inch baking dish and place in oven while it preheats (works best not to use a glass dish).

In a large mixing bowl, stir together the flour, cornmeal, cheese, baking soda, baking powder and salt. Set aside.

In another bowl, whisk together the egg, buttermilk, water, oil and chopped onion. Pour into the flour mixture all at once and stir until thoroughly blended. Pour the batter into the hot baking pan and bake for about 25 minutes, or until a tester inserted in the middle comes out clean. Cut into 10 squares and serve warm.

HIGH ALTITUDE No adjustments are necessary.

desserts

Palisade Peach Pie **page 224**

I've long admired Ina Garten of the Barefoot Contessa; she once said that people may enjoy your main course, but they always remember the dessert! I couldn't agree more. In the Clayton household, Dad insisted on having ice cream, at least, after dinner. Mom was a cookie-aholic. I tend to prefer desserts with lemon or fruit. Of course, we all love chocolate. No matter what suits your fancy, you'll be sure to find the perfect ending among our dessert recipes.

Fast Fruit Cobbler

SERVES 6 TO 8

Fruit cobbler has been around, in various forms, for years. Cobblers have become American favorites because they're easy to make and always so satisfying. My favorite way to make one uses a mix of blueberries and raspberries. Mom also liked to make this cobbler recipe with canned apple pie filling, to serve at the end of a hearty fall dinner.

1 can (16 ounce) crushed pineapple, drained
2 cups fresh blueberries (or mix of blueberries and raspberries) – can also substitute 1 can of apple, cherry or blueberry pie filling
1 package yellow cake mix (Jiffy works well)
½ cup chopped pecans
1½ sticks butter, melted

Preheat oven to 350 degrees. Grease a 7x11-inch baking dish.

In the prepared baking dish, layer all of the ingredients in the pan, beginning with the pineapple on the bottom, then the berries, then the cake mix and finish with the chopped nuts. Drizzle the melted butter over the top. Bake for 1 hour. Best served warm or at room temperature but not hot. Serve with vanilla ice cream.

MAKE AHEAD Cobbler can be made earlier in the day, covered and held at room temperature

Palisade Peach Pie

SERVES 8 TO 10

●

Every September we look forward to the delicious peaches from Palisade, Colorado. I like desserts that I can make ahead for entertaining, so I set out to find a method for making peach pie and freezing it so that the fresh flavor of the peaches is preserved yet the crust doesn't get soggy after baking. After much research, I decided that the best method is to freeze the crust and filling separately. At the end of the directions we explain how to make the pie if you want to bake it immediately. Use this freezing method for any fruit-filled pie. *(Photo, page 220)*

CRUSTS
2 cups all purpose flour, sifted
¾ teaspoon salt
2 tablespoons granulated sugar
½ cup unsalted butter, chilled,
   cut up into small pieces
3 tablespoons shortening
   (we like to use Crisco),
   cut up into small pieces
1 large egg
5 to 6 tablespoons ice water,
   divided
½ cup ground almonds

PIE FILLING
2¼ pounds medium-sized ripe
   peaches, peeled and sliced
   ¼- to ⅜-inch thick
½ cup dried cranberries
Juice of 1 lemon
½ to ¾ cup granulated sugar
   (depends on sweetness of
   peaches)
⅛ teaspoon nutmeg
⅛ teaspoon cinnamon
⅛ teaspoon mace
3 tablespoons cornstarch
2 tablespoons unsalted butter,
   cut up into small pieces
1 egg, beaten for egg glaze

To make the crust

Place the flour, salt and sugar in the bowl of a food processor fitted with the steel blade. Cover and pulse 2 or 3 times to mix the dry ingredients. Add the cut up butter and shortening and process 5 to 10 seconds until the dough has the texture of rough cornmeal. Add egg and 3 tablespoons of ice water and pulse 2 to 3 times. Add ground nuts and 2 tablespoons of ice water and pulse 2 to 3 times. Watch the dough carefully and stop the machine as soon as the dough starts to clump together. It will look rough and lumpy and there may still be unincorporated pieces of butter and egg. If it looks too dry and crumbly, sprinkle in a little more water and pulse 1 more time. Pinch the dough together with your fingers; if the dough holds together, it is done. Do not allow the dough to form a ball on the machine blades as it will be overworked and tough.

Turn dough out onto a piece of wax paper. Form the dough into 2 balls of the same size, wrap and refrigerate for at least 20 minutes (or up to several hours). On a lightly floured work surface, roll one ball of dough into a 12-inch circle. Sandwich the pastry round between two pieces of wax paper set on cardboard backing or large cookie sheet. Repeat with second ball of dough. Wrap tightly in aluminum foil and freeze (if using a cookie sheet for support, wrap dough in foil, then set on sheet; remove cookie sheet once crusts are frozen).

To make the pie filling

In a large mixing bowl, toss the peaches with the cranberries, lemon juice, sugar, nutmeg, cinnamon, mace and cornstarch.

To freeze the filling

Center a 12x24-inch piece of foil over a 9-inch pie plate. Mound the peach mixture on the foil over the pie plate and pat it down into the dish. Sprinkle the pieces of butter over the top. Fold up the foil, pushing out the excess air to seal. Leave in the pie plate and freeze. Once frozen you can remove the pie plate and leave the filling in the freezer.

To assemble and bake the pie after freezing

Preheat oven to 425 degrees.

Thaw the pie crusts for about 10 to 15 minutes. Don't thaw the filling. Line a 9-inch pie plate with one of the crusts. Brush with egg glaze (1 egg beaten with 1 tablespoon of water). Place the peach filling (frozen) inside the crust. Cut steam vents in the top crust, moisten the edges of the bottom crust, then place on the top crust. Fold the edges of the top crust over the lower one and pinch to seal. Mold the edges into a fluted rim. Bake in the lower third of the oven for 25 minutes. Reduce heat to 350 degrees, raise pie to center of oven, cover pastry edges with foil and continue baking for another 35 minutes or until bubbly and light brown on top.

To assemble and bake the pie immediately

Line a 9-inch pie plate with one of the crusts. Brush with egg glaze (1 egg beaten with 1 tablespoon of water). Place the peach filling inside the crust. Sprinkle the pieces of butter over the top. Cut steam vents in the top crust, moisten the edges of the bottom crust, then place on the top crust. Fold the edges of the top crust over the lower one and pinch to seal. Mold the edges into a fluted rim. Bake for 10 minutes in bottom third of oven at 425 degrees, followed by 35 to 40 minutes in the center of the oven at 350 degrees. Place foil on crust if it looks like it is browning too fast.

Blueberry Tart

SERVES 8

Our family friend Izzie Bowman (who gave Mom this recipe) originally called this "Very Rich" Blueberry Tart. Once you see the butter and sugar in this recipe, you'll know why! This is a perfect entertaining dessert as it can be made ahead and frozen until serving.

14 tablespoons butter at room temperature, divided
1⅓ cups honey graham cracker crumbs (about 20 squares)
2 tablespoons light brown sugar
1 cup granulated sugar
24 ounces fresh blueberries (about 1¾ to 2 cups)
1 cup powdered sugar
2 large eggs
1 teaspoon vanilla
1½ cups heavy cream

Preheat oven to 350 degrees.

Melt 6 tablespoons of the butter and mix into the graham cracker crumbs along with the brown sugar. Press into bottom and sides of a 9-inch tart pan (or pie pan). Bake for 6 to 8 minutes. Cool.

In a medium saucepan, stir together 1 cup granulated sugar and 1/2 cup water. Bring to a boil, add berries and cook until juice is reduced and thick. Cool and chill.

With an electric mixer, beat 8 tablespoons butter and very gradually add powdered sugar. When light and fluffy, add eggs, one at a time, beating well after each addition. Beat in vanilla. Pour into prepared crust. Top with blueberry mixture. Cover and freeze.

Remove tart from freezer when serving main course. Beat heavy cream until stiff. Don't sweeten the cream—this dessert has enough sugar already! Cover tart with whipped cream just before serving.

VARIATION For a faster version, substitute 2 cans (15 ounce) blueberry pie mix in place of 2 pints blueberries and 1 cup granulated sugar and 1/2 cup water. Spread over top of butter-sugar mixture.

MAKE AHEAD Tart can be made up to 1 month ahead and kept frozen.

Rhubarb Pie

SERVES 6 (1 9-INCH PIE)

●

Rhubarb pie is always a favorite in our family. Mom grew rhubarb in her garden every summer to make sure she'd always have enough to make this pie. She preferred using only rhubarb rather than the popular version of this pie that also includes strawberries.

3 eggs, beaten
2⅔ tablespoons whole milk
2 tablespoons melted butter, cooled
4 cups chopped peeled rhubarb stalks
1¾ to 2 cups sugar
4 tablespoons flour
¾ teaspoon nutmeg
2 prepared 9-inch pie crusts (top and bottom), uncooked

Preheat oven to 400 degrees.

In a small mixing bowl, whisk together the eggs, milk and melted butter. Set aside. In a large mixing bowl, stir together the rhubarb, sugar, flour and nutmeg. Add the liquid ingredients and stir to mix.

Place one pie crust in 9-inch pie pan. Spread rhubarb mixture evenly. Make a lattice top with second crust and place on top, sealing edges. Bake for 40 to 60 minutes. Cover edge with foil if it browns too fast.

NOTE Use only the stalks of rhubarb, never the leaves as they are poisonous.

Captain Lee's Kentucky Bourbon Apple Pie

SERVES 8 (1 9-INCH PIE)

●

This classic recipe comes from Mom's brother, Dan Lee. Uncle Dan loved to cook and this was a signature recipe of his—no doubt because it features his favorite ingredient, bourbon! Different from most apple pies, this one doesn't have a top crust.

6 Granny Smith or Golden apples, peeled, cored and sliced very thin
Lots of Kentucky bourbon
1 9-inch pie crust, using Kentucky bourbon in place of the water when making
1 cup dark brown sugar
Dash salt
2 tablespoons cornstarch
½ teaspoon allspice

Place the apples in a pie dish and pour in enough bourbon to cover the apples. Cover with another dish, place a weighted plate on top and soak apples overnight.

Preheat oven to 425 degrees. Lightly spray a 9-inch pie plate with cooking spray.

Place the pie crust in the prepared pie plate. Prick the bottom.

Whisk together the sugar, salt, cornstarch and allspice. With a large slotted spoon (to avoid excessive draining of the bourbon), put the bourbon-soaked apple slices in the sugar mixture, and carefully stir to ensure each slice is coated. Place apple slices in overlapping pattern around the outer edge of the pie, continuing this design to the center. Layer the same way until all slices are used. Bake for 20 to 25 minutes (never more) until apple slices are tender. Crust may need to be covered with foil if browning too fast. Remove from oven, cool to room temperature then cool completely in the refrigerator. Top with whipped cream (flavored with bourbon, of course).

VARIATION Add green food coloring and mint extract to whipping cream, and you now have Kentucky Mint Julep Apple Pie.

Derby Pie

●

Mom says it's not Kentucky Derby Day unless Derby Pie is served. This pie is an old Kentucky recipe that is basically a rich pecan pie with chocolate chips.

1 unbaked 9-inch pie shell
2 eggs, slightly beaten
½ cup sugar
½ cup light Karo syrup
½ cup flour
½ cup butter, melted and cooled
1 cup pecan halves
1 cup chocolate chips
1 teaspoon vanilla

Preheat oven to 375 degrees.

Combine all pie ingredients and spread evenly in pie shell. Bake at 375 degrees for 10 minutes, then turn heat down to 350 degrees and continue baking for an additional 35 minutes. Let cool some before slicing. Can be served warm or at room temperature. Serve with whipped cream or vanilla ice cream.

Fluffy Pumpkin Pie

SERVES 8 TO 10 (1 10-INCH DEEP DISH PIE)

I first discovered this recipe more than 20 years ago, when my college roommate Cynthia was recently married and we decided to cook our first complete Thanksgiving dinner on our own. This pie is so fluffy, light and full of flavor—I have yet to find another that tastes better. For a prettier presentation, I recently added the decorative whipped topping, but you can just serve whipped cream on the side if you prefer.

Favorite pie dough, enough for
   one crust of a 10-inch deep dish
   pie dish
1 can (15 ounce) cooked pumpkin
½ cup light brown sugar, packed
½ cup sugar
½ teaspoon salt
1½ tablespoons molasses
1½ tablespoons good dark rum (or
   bourbon)
1½ teaspoons cinnamon
1½ teaspoons ginger
⅛ teaspoon nutmeg
⅛ teaspoon cloves
2 egg yolks
½ cup heavy cream
6 tablespoons whole milk
3 egg whites
1 tablespoon sugar

OPTIONAL DECORATIVE TOPPING
2 cups whipping cream
1 tablespoon good dark rum (or
   bourbon)
2 tablespoons powdered sugar
ground cinnamon (for dusting)

Preheat oven to 450 degrees. Line a 10-inch deep dish pie plate with the pie crust, making a strong fluted rim that extends about 1/2-inch above the rim of the dish. (If you are using purchased refrigerated pie crust, you will need to roll it out a bit to make it slightly larger.) Do not prick the bottom of the pastry.

Using an electric mixer, blend together the pumpkin, sugars, salt, molasses, rum, cinnamon, ginger, nutmeg, cloves, egg yolks, cream and milk just until mixed. Set aside. In another bowl, beat the egg whites until foamy. Add a pinch of salt and continue beating to form soft peaks. With the mixer running, slowly add 1 tablespoon of sugar and continue beating to form stiff, shiny peaks. Stir 1/4 of the egg whites into the pumpkin mixture, then fold in the rest just until mixed. Immediately pour into the pie shell, filling only to the rim of the pan.

Immediately bake the pie for 15 minutes. When the rim of the crust just starts to brown, reduce the heat to 375 degrees and continue baking for another 15 minutes—lower heat if the pastry is browning too much. Lower the heat again to 350 degrees and continue baking for another 15 minutes, or until filling 2 inches from the edge is done (an inserted toothpick will come out clean). Turn off oven, leave the door open and let the pie sit in the oven for another 20 to 30 minutes. You need to watch this pie carefully so that it doesn't cook too fast—if it does, it will get watery.

Optional decorative topping

Once the pie is at room temperature, beat the cream, rum and sugar until very stiff. Cut the corner off of a ziploc baggie, fit a large star tip into the corner and fill the bag with the whipped cream. Pipe 1-inch stars on top of the pie, starting with one in the center and making circles around it. Lightly dust the top with ground cinnamon. Cover and refrigerate until ready to serve.

NOTE To keep plastic wrap or foil from mushing the whipped cream stars when you cover the pie, place toothpicks all around the pie—they will hold the cover away from the surface of the pie. You will likely have some whipped cream left over—we refrigerate it and serve it with Kim and Jan's Pecan Pie.

MAKE AHEAD The pie can be made up to one day ahead, the topping added earlier during the day of serving.

Kim and Jan's Pecan Pie

SERVES 8 (1 9-INCH PIE)

●

This recipe comes from Kim Moore and her partner, Jan. After just one bite of this pie Mom tossed out her old recipe. This is the best we've ever had!

1 9-inch unbaked pie shell
1 cup pecan halves
3 eggs
1 cup light Karo syrup
1 cup light brown sugar
2 tablespoons butter, melted
1 teaspoon vanilla
½ teaspoon salt

Preheat oven to 400 degrees.

Spread the pecan halves evenly over the bottom of the pie shell. Set aside.

In a large mixing bowl, whisk together the eggs, Karo syrup, sugar, butter, vanilla and salt. Evenly pour mixture over pecans. Bake for 15 minutes, then reduce oven temperature to 350 degrees and cook for an additional 45 minutes. Turn the oven off and let the pie rest in the oven for 10 to 15 minutes. Serve warm or at room temperature, with vanilla ice cream or whipped cream.

Lemon Custard Cups

SERVES 6 TO 8

●

Another wonderful recipe from my grandmother, Nama. Note that the number of ramekins you need (and therefore the total number of servings) depends on their size. If you are using 4-ounce ramekins, then you will need 8. We think that 6-ounce ramekins make the best serving size.

2 tablespoons butter
Zest from 1 lemon
5 tablespoons fresh lemon juice
1 cup sugar
¼ cup flour
Pinch salt
2 eggs, separated
1½ cups milk

Preheat oven to 350 degrees. Butter 6 to 8 custard cups or ramekins.

With an electric mixer using a whisk attachment, beat the butter until creamy. Beat in lemon zest and lemon juice. Whisk together the sugar, flour and salt and beat into mixture. Whisk together 2 egg yolks and milk; stir by hand into mixture. Set aside.

Beat 2 egg whites until stiff. Fold 1/4 of beaten egg whites into custard. Fold in remaining whites. Divide custard mixture equally among prepared ramekins (they should be almost full). Place in a large baking dish or roasting pan. Pour very hot water into baking dish to come halfway up sides of ramekins. Bake for 45 minutes or until golden brown. Remove from the water bath to a wire rack, bring to room temperature, then cover and chill until serving time.

MAKE AHEAD Custard cups can be made 1 day ahead and stored, covered, in the refrigerator.

Kahlúa Chocolate Mousse

SERVES 6

●

This is a divine chocolate mousse that features Kahlúa and orange flavor. It is perfectly wonderful on its own or with whipped cream on top.

6 ounces semi-sweet chocolate
 chips
2 tablespoons Kahlúa liqueur
1 tablespoon fresh orange juice
2 eggs
2 egg yolks
1 teaspoon vanilla
¼ cup extra fine sugar
1 cup heavy cream

In the top of a double boiler over low heat (water at a low boil), cook the chocolate chips and Kahlúa, stirring, just until the chocolate is melted. Set aside to cool a bit. Don't worry if it comes out looking like a ganache—it will still work.

In a blender container or food processor bowl, combine the orange juice, eggs, egg yolks, vanilla and sugar. Blend. Add melted chocolate mixture and blend again. Add heavy cream and blend again. Pour into six pots de crème or stemmed glasses. Refrigerate at least 4 hours before serving.

MAKE AHEAD Mousse can be made 24 hours ahead, covered and refrigerated.

Eggnog and White Chocolate Pots de Crème

SERVES 6

I have a large collection of pots de crème, most of which cannot go in the oven, so I am always looking for (or creating) recipes for them that don't need to be baked. This dessert takes very little time to prepare and is a wonderful, light ending to a holiday meal. If you don't have pots de crème, you can use wine glasses, demitasse cups or ramekins.

2 cups purchased eggnog
1 teaspoon unflavored gelatin
¼ teaspoon ground cinnamon
⅛ teaspoon ground nutmeg
3 ounces chopped white chocolate
  (or white chocolate chips)
3 tablespoons brandy (or dark rum)
1 teaspoon vanilla

Place eggnog in a medium saucepan and stir in gelatin, cinnamon and nutmeg. Place over medium heat and cook, stirring, until steaming, about 7 minutes. Remove from heat and stir in chocolate, brandy and vanilla, stirring until chocolate is melted (takes up to 5 minutes). Divide mixture among 6 pots de crème (about ½ cup each). Cover with plastic wrap (making sure it doesn't touch the top of the eggnog mixture). Chill until softly set, at least 4 hours or up to 1 day. Garnish with brandy (or rum) flavored whipped cream.

MAKE AHEAD Pots de crème can be made up to 24 hours ahead, covered and refrigerated.

Apple Cake

SERVES 8 TO 10

My brother Jim and I always loved this apple cake as kids. Today, I love to serve it at the end of a casual dinner or as part of a picnic at a Denver Botanic Gardens concert. The recipe originally came from Mom's cousin Mary Pryor in Kentucky.

3½ cups peeled and chopped tart apples
2 cups sugar
3 cups flour
2 teaspoons baking soda
½ teaspoon cinnamon
½ teaspoon allspice
½ teaspoon cloves
½ teaspoon nutmeg
1 cup chopped walnuts
1 cup + 1 tablespoon melted butter, divided
2 eggs, beaten
1 teaspoon vanilla
1 cup powdered sugar
1 tablespoon light corn syrup
1 tablespoon milk

Preheat the oven to 375 degrees. Grease a 9x13-inch baking dish or a large tube pan.

In a large mixing bowl, combine the chopped apples and 2 cups sugar. Set aside.

Sift together the flour, baking soda, cinnamon, allspice, cloves and nutmeg. In a small mixing bowl, toss together the walnuts and 1 tablespoon of the flour mixture. Set both aside.

To the apple mixture, add 1 cup of the melted butter and stir until combined. Stir in the eggs and vanilla. Add the flour mixture and stir just until combined. Fold in the walnuts (and any flour mixture in the bowl). Spread evenly in the prepared dish and bake for 1 hour. Cool in pan to lukewarm.

While the cake is baking, make the glaze. Stir together the remaining 1 tablespoon of melted butter, the powdered sugar, light corn syrup and milk. Spread over the top of the lukewarm cake. Let cool until the glaze is set before serving.

MAKE AHEAD Cake will keep for several days, covered and refrigerated.

HIGH ALTITUDE Decrease sugar by 2 tablespoons, reduce baking soda by 1/4 teaspoon, increase butter by 1 tablespoon and use extra large eggs.

Jam Cake with Caramel Frosting

SERVES 8 TO 10

This is a traditional Kentucky dessert, dating back more than 100 years. It was Mom's favorite cake as a child—and she loved it throughout her life, especially on her birthday!

CAKE
1½ cups flour
½ teaspoon baking soda
½ teaspoon allspice
½ teaspoon cinnamon
½ teaspoon nutmeg
½ teaspoon cloves
⅛ teaspoon salt
1 tablespoon cocoa powder
1 cup sugar
½ cup butter
½ teaspoon vanilla
2 eggs
½ cup blackberry jam*
½ cup buttermilk
½ cup raisins
½ cup chopped pecans (optional)

CARAMEL FROSTING
½ cup butter
1 cup light brown sugar
½ cup whole milk
1 teaspoon vanilla
1½ to 2 cups powdered sugar

Use any flavor jam, but blackberry is the traditional ingredient

To make the cake: preheat oven to 350 degrees. Butter and flour two 8-inch round cake pans.

In a medium bowl, sift together the flour, baking soda, allspice, cinnamon, nutmeg, cloves, salt and cocoa powder. Set aside.

With an electric mixer, cream the sugar, butter and vanilla until light and fluffy. With the mixer running, add the eggs one at a time, beating well and scraping the bowl after each addition. Blend in jam. Add half of the dry ingredient mixture, then half the buttermilk. Repeat and mix just until blended. Stop the mixer and fold in raisins and pecans. Pour batter into prepared pans and bake for about 25 to 30 minutes or until a tester inserted into the center of the pan comes out clean. Place pans on a wire rack to cool.

To make the frosting: in a medium saucepan, melt the butter over low heat. Stir in the brown sugar and cook 2 minutes. Whisk in the milk and bring to a boil, stirring constantly. Take off heat and stir in vanilla, then powdered sugar until the right consistency—thick enough to ice the cake but not lumpy. Let cool to room temperature before icing the cake.

Assembly

If the cakes have domed out on the top, cut the top of the dome off so each section of cake is fairly flat on the top. Place one cake layer on the serving platter you plan to use. (Note: If you place pieces of wax paper around the edge of the serving platter and then put the cake on top, the paper will catch any frosting that drips when you ice the cake. You can then gently pull them out after you are done and this way the serving platter stays clean.) Spread some of the frosting on the top, about 1/4-inch thick. Take the second cake layer and place it upside down on top of the icing (this way the smoothest side, which is the bottom during baking, is the top of your cake). Ice the top and sides with remaining frosting.

NOTE This recipe can be doubled, using three 9-inch cake pans.

HIGH ALTITUDE No adjustments are necessary.

Robert E. Lee Cake

SERVES 12 TO 14

This cake is a recipe from my maternal grandmother, Nama (known to others as Bessie Lee). It was one of her—and our—favorites, which is why we have included it in this book even though it takes more time than our other recipes. Despite that, it's definitely worth the effort. You will need a total of 8 lemons and 4 large navel oranges for this recipe. Zest the lemons and oranges first, before juicing—it is much easer this way.

LEMON CURD FILLING
6 tablespoons butter
¾ cup fresh lemon juice
¾ cup sugar
6 egg yolks
4 teaspoons fresh lemon zest

LEMON CAKE
2 cups flour
1 teaspoon baking powder
½ teaspoon salt
8 eggs, separated
2 cups sugar
¼ cup fresh lemon juice
2 teaspoons fresh lemon zest

ORANGE-LEMON FROSTING
¼ cup fresh orange juice
2 tablespoons fresh lemon juice
8 tablespoons butter
4½ cups powdered sugar
    (or more if needed to thicken)
1 egg yolk
¼ cup fresh orange zest
2 teaspoons fresh lemon zest

Preheat oven to 350 degrees. Butter and flour two 9-inch round cake pans.

For the filling
Cut butter into bits. Mix butter, lemon juice, sugar and egg yolks in a medium saucepan and cook over low heat, stirring constantly until thick. Scrape out into a medium mixing bowl and stir in lemon zest. Cool, then refrigerate for at least 30 minutes.

For the cake
In a medium mixing bowl, sift together the flour, baking powder and salt. Set aside. Beat together the 8 egg yolks and sugar with the whisk attachment of a mixer for 4 to 5 minutes or until creamy and light yellow. Beat in lemon juice and lemon zest until blended. Add flour mixture, 1/2 cup at a time, beating just until mixed.

In a separate bowl, beat the 8 egg whites until stiff. Fold into the batter. Divide the batter evenly between the two prepared pans; smooth the tops. Bake for 35 minutes or until a toothpick inserted into the center comes out clean. Cool 5 minutes in the pan, then turn out onto racks to cool completely.

For the frosting
Mix together the orange and lemon juices. Set aside. With an electric mixer, beat butter until creamy and a light yellow color. Beat in the powdered sugar and juice mixture, alternating 1/3 of the mixture at a time. Beat in egg yolk. Stir in orange and lemon zests. If it isn't very thick, refrigerate frosting until it thickens— otherwise it will run off the sides of the cake.

Assembly

Cut each cake in half horizontally so you have 4 rounds. Place one cake piece on a cake plate, cut side up. Spread 1/3 of filling mixture on top, leaving a 1/8-inch margin free around the sides. Repeat 2 more times. Place final cake round, cut side down, on the top. If your cake pieces aren't even, you can use the lemon curd filling to make it level. Frost top and sides—again, using the frosting to make the top level.

HIGH ALTITUDE For the cake, reduce the baking powder by 1/8 teaspoon, increase lemon juice by 1/4 to 1/2 teaspoon, and use extra large eggs. Do not increase oven temperature.

A well-seasoned memory

*M*om *always took care of us, so on her birthday, it was always a treat to cook for her. One birthday celebration, I prepared a strawberry soufflé for dessert. I completely misread the recipe, cooking the dessert for 45 minutes instead of the requisite 25 minutes. Let me tell you—overcooking a soufflé creates quite a mess! Instead of a dish for 10, there was enough for maybe four people. But, after years of watching my Mom, I knew exactly how to save the night. I had cookies in the freezer that I quick-thawed in the microwave. I scooped out what was left of the soufflé onto each plate, added a side of cookies and created a perfect little dessert. No one was the wiser and Mom had a great celebratory dinner.*

Sally cooking up another delicious meal.

Pavlova

SERVES 8

●

Mom was first introduced to this dessert, named after the Russian ballerina, by friends in Australia. It has been a family favorite for years and has been served on many a birthday by request. While the instructions appear long, it is not difficult to make and can be made in stages. If you don't have the time or energy to make the sauce, don't worry—it is just as good without it!

MERINGUE
1 cup sugar, divided
1½ teaspoons cornstarch
4 egg whites
¼ teaspoon salt
¼ teaspoon cream of tartar
1½ teaspoons white wine vinegar
1 teaspoon vanilla

TOPPING
2 cups whipping cream
¼ cup sugar
¼ cup vanilla flavored brandy or
    Grand Marnier
¼ teaspoon vanilla
Mixture of blueberries,
    blackberries, raspberries,
    sliced strawberries and
    peeled, sliced kiwi

SAUCE (OPTIONAL)
1 tablespoon cornstarch
½ cup sugar
Dash salt
½ cup water
3 teaspoon lemon juice
¼ teaspoon vanilla
1 package (10 ounce) frozen
    unsweetened raspberries
    (if sweetened, reduce
    amount of sugar)

To make the meringue

Preheat the oven to 400 degrees. Line a large cookie sheet with parchment paper and draw a 10-inch circle in the middle.

In a small bowl, mix together 1 tablespoon of the sugar and the cornstarch and set aside.

With an electric mixer on high, beat the egg whites, salt and cream of tartar together until just frothy. With the machine running, start adding the remaining sugar to the egg white mixture, 1 tablespoon at a time. Next add the sugar-cornstarch mixture, then the vinegar and vanilla. Beat until the mixture is glossy and forms stiff peaks. Try not to overbeat, as the meringue doesn't come out right if the mixture gets dry.

Using a spatula, spread the meringue mixture within the circle on your parchment, stopping 1 inch inside the border. Spread it slightly higher around the edges than in the middle. Place in the preheated oven, then immediately turn the temperature down to 250 degrees. Bake for 1 hour, or until lightly browned and dry on the surface. Remove the meringue from the oven—don't be worried if it cracks. Cool completely. Wrap airtight with plastic wrap and store at room temperature until ready to use (up to 24 hours).

To make the topping and assemble

With an electric mixer, beat the whipping cream, sugar, liquor and vanilla until stiff peaks form. Just before serving, spread the whipped cream mixture over the meringue, covering it completely (you may have some left over). Spread the fruit over the top in a decorative pattern. Spoon a small amount of the sauce on the side of each serving if desired (not too much— it is very sweet).

Strawberry and White Chocolate Heaven

SERVES 10

This dessert is true to its name—it's a little taste of heaven. And, it's much lighter than it reads. For a large crowd, double the recipe and put it in a 12-inch springform pan. Definitely use only fresh strawberries as they're the star of the show. Besides, frozen strawberries tend to have a lot of juice which can run out of the bottom of the springform pan.

1 cup **Nilla Vanilla cookie crumbs**
½ cup **finely chopped, toasted almonds**
¼ cup **butter, melted**
4 cups **fresh whole strawberries, washed and dried**
12 ounces **white chocolate, coarsely chopped**
4 ounces **cream cheese, softened**
¼ cup **sugar**
¼ cup **Grand Marnier (can substitute orange juice concentrate)**
1 teaspoon **vanilla**
2 cups **whipping cream**
Cocoa powder

In a medium mixing bowl, combine the cookie crumbs, almonds and butter. Press into the bottom of a 9-inch springform pan. Cut the stems off the strawberries. Cut enough in half lengthwise to press flat around the entire side of the springform pan, arranging with points up. Place remaining whole berries, points up, on crust, filling the pan. Set aside.

In the top of a double boiler over low heat (water at a low boil), melt the chocolate. Set aside to cool slightly. With an electric mixer, beat the cream cheese until smooth. Beat in sugar, then Grand Marnier and vanilla. With the beaters running, slowly add the melted chocolate.

In a separate bowl, whip the cream until peaks form. Stir 1/3 of the whipped cream into the chocolate mixture, then fold in the rest. Pour over strawberries, making sure to fill in between berries. Cover and refrigerate at least 3 hours or overnight. Remove sides of pan. Dust top with cocoa powder.

MAKE AHEAD The dessert can be made up to 1 day ahead, covered and refrigerated. It can also be frozen for up to 1 month.

Frozen Peppermint Cheesecake

SERVES 12

This recipe came from our friend Nancy Jones who serves it nearly every year on Christmas Eve to her extended family. It is great for holiday entertaining as it can be made up to a month ahead of time.

1½ cups chocolate wafer crumbs
¼ cup sugar
¼ cup butter
8 ounces cream cheese, softened
1 can (14 ounce) sweetened condensed milk
1 cup crushed hard peppermint candy
½ cup mini chocolate chips
2 cups whipping cream

Combine cookie crumbs, sugar and butter. Firmly press into bottom of either a 9-inch springform pan or a 9x13-inch pan. Chill.

Beat cream cheese at high speed with an electric mixer until fluffy. Add condensed milk and beat well. Stir in peppermint candy and chocolate chips. Whip cream and fold into mixture. Pour into prepared pan and freeze until firm (at least 4 hours, preferably overnight). Garnish with whipped cream and peppermint candies if desired.

If you're feeling really creative, make a poinsettia in the middle with chocolate leaves, placing crushed peppermint candies in the middle.

MAKE AHEAD This dessert can be made up to a month ahead and kept frozen.

Frozen Brandy Alexander Pie

SERVES 10

●

My husband Robert and I love frozen Brandy Alexander drinks so much we served them at our wedding reception after dinner. In seeking new ways to use the flavors of our favorite drink, I created this recipe one Christmas and everyone loved it.

1 cup graham cracker crumbs
1½ tablespoons cinnamon
¼ cup butter, melted
2 quarts good quality vanilla ice cream, softened
6 to 8 tablespoons brandy
6 to 8 tablespoons crème de cacao
Ground nutmeg

In a medium mixing bowl, combine the graham cracker crumbs and cinnamon. Mix in the melted butter with your hands. Press into the bottom of a 9-inch springform pan.

With an electric blender, blend together the ice cream, brandy and crème de cacao. You may need to do this in batches, depending on the size of your blender. Pour into the prepared crust, cover and freeze overnight. Sprinkle top with nutmeg before serving.

This dessert only needs to sit a room temperature a few minutes before cutting—the alcohol keeps it from freezing very hard.

MAKE AHEAD The dessert can be made up to 1 month ahead and kept in the freezer.

Lemon Almond Ice Cream

MAKES 2 QUARTS; SERVES ABOUT 12

This ice cream is just the right mix of sweet and tart. I remember Mom making this for dinner parties when we were growing up. It is still a favorite today. Serve it in Sally's Pecan Cookie Cups topped with raspberries and blueberries for a real treat!

4 cups half and half
1½ cups granulated sugar
grated rind from 2½ lemons
½ cup lemon juice
½ cup toasted slivered almonds
½ teaspoon vanilla
¼ teaspoon almond extract

Mix all ingredients, put in ice cream freezer and process until firm. Note that some ice cream freezers recommend adding ingredients such as the almonds later in the cycle. Check the instructions for your machine.

MAKE AHEAD Ice cream can be made up to 2 months ahead and kept in the freezer.

Sally's Pecan Cookie Cups

SERVES 12

A favorite at Mom's dinner parties, these cookie cups can be filled with ice cream, sorbet or mousse and fresh berries.

¼ cup unsalted butter
¼ cup packed light brown sugar
¼ cup light corn syrup
3½ tablespoons flour
½ cup finely chopped pecans
1 teaspoon vanilla

Preheat oven to 325 degrees. Grease and flour several large cookie sheets.

In a medium saucepan, melt butter over low heat. Add brown sugar and corn syrup. Heat to boiling, stirring constantly. Remove from heat and stir in flour and chopped pecans. Stir in vanilla.

Place 2 to 3 teaspoons of the batter on baking sheet and smooth slightly. Repeat with remaining mixture, spacing about 6 inches apart (about 3 cookies will fit on one large sheet). Bake 10 to 12 minutes or until golden brown. Remove from oven and let cool on the cookie sheet for 1 minute, then invert each cookie over a deep ramekin or custard cup (you can also use an inverted muffin tin). Press down gently to form a cup. Repeat with each cookie. You need to do this quickly before the cookies start to harden on the sheet. Cool for 5 minutes and then gently remove to a rack to cool completely. Note that these cookies are very fragile and you are likely to break a few during the shaping process or when you fill them.

MAKE AHEAD The cookies can be made one day ahead and stored in an airtight container at room temperature.

Cheesecake Squares

Growing up, we loved Mom's Cheesecake Squares. The only problem is that the recipe was lost somewhere during the process of compiling this cookbook. After some Internet research along with some experimenting, we finally hit on what Mom and I both thought was her original recipe.

½ cup butter, softened
⅓ cup packed brown sugar
1 cup flour
½ cup finely chopped pecans
¼ cup sugar
8 ounces cream cheese, softened
1 egg, beaten
2 tablespoons fresh lemon juice
1 teaspoon lemon zest
2 tablespoons whole milk
½ teaspoon vanilla

Preheat oven to 350 degrees. Lightly butter an 8x8-inch baking dish.

With an electric mixer using a whisk attachment, cream together the butter and brown sugar until well blended. Place the flour and nuts in the bowl, turn on low, slowly increasing speed to incorporate. You will need to stop a few times and scrape the sides and bottom of the bowl. Mixture should resemble coarse crumbs. Reserve 1/2 cup mixture for topping. Press remaining crumb mixture into the bottom of the prepared baking dish. Bake for 10 to 12 minutes or until lightly browned.

While the crust is baking

Again using an electric mixer with whisk attachment, blend together the sugar and cream cheese until creamy and smooth. With the machine running, add the egg, then the lemon juice, zest, milk and vanilla. Beat until well mixed, scraping down the sides as needed. Pour mixture evenly over the hot baked crust and sprinkle the reserved crumb mixture over the top. Bake for 20 to 23 minutes. It will puff up and then settle back down. Cool to room temperature in the pan on a wire rack, then refrigerate.

Cut into 16 bars. Store, covered, in the refrigerator.

Layered Oatmeal Chocolate Bars

MAKES 3 DOZEN COOKIES

●

Mom used to like to make bar cookies because they are so quick to put together. These are very rich so we recommend cutting them into small pieces.

CHOCOLATE LAYER
2 tablespoons butter
6 ounces semi-sweet chocolate chips
1 small can (5 ounce) evaporated milk
¼ cup sugar
½ cup chopped pecans

COOKIE LAYER
½ cup butter, softened
1 cup brown sugar, firmly packed
1 egg
1 teaspoon vanilla
1¼ cups flour
½ teaspoon baking soda
2 cups quick cooking oats, divided

Preheat oven to 350 degrees. Grease a 9-inch square baking pan (a 7x11-inch pan will also work).

First make the chocolate layer
In heavy saucepan over medium heat, combine the butter, chocolate chips, milk and sugar. Cook, stirring, until melted and mixed together. Remove from heat and stir in nuts. Set aside to cool while you make the cookie layer.

Cookie layer
With an electric mixer using the whisk attachment, cream together the butter and sugar. Add the egg and vanilla and continue beating until light and fluffy. In a separate mixing bowl, stir together the flour, baking soda and 1 3/4 cups of the oats. Beat into the butter mixture just until blended. Press 3/4 of the cookie dough into the bottom of the prepared pan, pushing down with moistened fingers into a tight, even layer. Spread the cooled chocolate mixture evenly over the top. Mix the remaining 1/4 cup oats into the remainder of the cookie dough. Sprinkle evenly over the chocolate layer.

Bake for 25 to 30 minutes.

Cool in pan on a wire rack to room temperature, then cover and refrigerate before cutting into 36 bars. Store in the refrigerator in an airtight container.

Nama's Lemon Love Notes

MAKES 24 TO 28

●

My maternal grandmother (dubbed Nama by my cousin Beth when she was a toddler) always loved these cookies and often made them for me and my brother when we would visit her in Tucson. They are decadently delicious!

COOKIES
½ cup butter, softened
1 cup flour
¼ cup powdered sugar
2 eggs
1 cup sugar
2 tablespoons fresh lemon juice
1 tablespoon fresh lemon zest
  (about 1 lemon)
½ teaspoon baking powder
¼ teaspoon salt

FROSTING
1 tablespoon butter, melted
¾ cup powdered sugar
1 tablespoon whole milk (or more)
½ teaspoon vanilla

Preheat oven to 350 degrees (or 325 if you are using a glass baking dish).

For the cookies

With an electric mixer, blend together the butter, flour and powdered sugar until the mixture resembles coarse meal. Press into the bottom of an ungreased 7x11-inch baking dish, and bake for 15 minutes. Set aside to cool (don't turn the oven off).

Again with the electric mixer, beat the eggs and sugar together just until light and fluffy. Add the lemon juice, lemon zest, baking powder and salt and blend until just mixed. Spread over top of cooked crust and bake for 25 minutes or until set (will puff up and then settle back down again). Set aside to cool in the pan for at least one hour before frosting.

For the frosting

In a small mixing bowl, stir all ingredients together until frosting consistency. Add more milk if too thick or more sugar if too thin. Spread over the top of the cookies. Refrigerate for at least one hour. Cut into bars (either 24 or 28, depending on how large you want the cookies to be).

Store the cookies in the pan until ready to serve, covered and refrigerated. Bring to room temperature before serving.

From left, clockwise: **Chocolate Coconut Pecan Bars, page 258**
Nama's Lemon Love Notes, page 252
Grandma Clayton's Sand Tarts, page 256

Almond Raspberry Valentine Cookies

MAKES AROUND 4 DOZEN

●

I created these cookies several years ago as gifts to provide single friends on Valentine's Day (I was also single at the time). For the last few years I made them for Mom on Valentines' Day, as she was a cookie lover. I have also made them at Christmas, cutting the cookie shape into small gingerbread men, but still cutting the interior shape as a heart.

1 package (14 ounce) blanched slivered (or whole) almonds
3⅓ cups cake flour
1 teaspoon baking powder
1 teaspoon ground cinnamon
1½ cups butter, room temperature
1 cup sugar
2 eggs
1 teaspoon vanilla extract
Good quality raspberry jam or preserves
Powdered sugar

Finely grind the almonds in a food processor; set aside. Sift together flour, baking powder and cinnamon in a medium mixing bowl; set aside.

Cream butter with an electric mixer until soft; gradually add sugar, beating until light and fluffy. Beat in eggs one at a time, then vanilla, beating until well mixed. Stir in ground almonds, then the flour mixture. Mix well. Divide dough into fourths, shaping into round, flat patties. Wrap in plastic wrap and refrigerate until firm—overnight is best. (But, if you are like me and not that organized, an hour may be enough; the longer it chills the easier the dough is to work with.)

Preheat oven to 350 degrees. Lightly grease 2 to 4 cookie sheets (depending on how many you have on hand).

Take one portion of the dough out of the refrigerator and roll between 2 pieces of waxed paper to 1/4- to 1/8-inch thickness. The thinner the better, but the dough becomes tricky to maneuver when it is really thin. (If you roll it to 1/4-inch thickness, you will end up with about 2 1/2 dozen cookies instead of 4 dozen.) Cut with a 2-inch heart-shaped cookie cutter and place half on one of the prepared cookie sheets. Cut out centers of remaining cookies with a small (1/4- to 1/2-inch) heart or circle shaped cookie cutter; place cookies on prepared cookie sheet. Re-roll leftover dough and continue cutting out cookies until all the dough is used. Bake cookies for 10 to 12 minutes or until lightly brown. Remove to wire rack to cool. Repeat procedure with remaining portions of dough that have been in the refrigerator.

Using a small spoon spread a small amount of raspberry jam (1/2 to 1 teaspoon) on the bottom side of each solid baked cookie. Top with cut out cookie, bottom side down, and press slightly to adhere. Sift powdered sugar over the top.

Store in airtight containers.

Chocolate Raspberry Valentine Cookies

Melt 6 ounces of semi-sweet chocolate chips in the microwave, making sure not to overcook (takes about a minute—even if they are not all melted, stir them and they will finish melting). Follow recipe as above, except before spreading the bottoms of the solid cookies with jam, using a small basting brush spread them first with the melted chocolate, then the jam.

Raspberry Christmas Cookies

Follow recipe as above except use a 2- to 3-inch gingerbread man cookie cutter instead of a heart shaped cutter. Center cut-out can still be a small heart or circle.

NOTE When cookie dough is rolled really thin, it can be tricky to pick up and transfer cut-out cookies to the cookie sheet. Try this: roll the dough out between two sheets of waxed paper to your preferred thickness, cut out all your cookies and try picking up one. If it doesn't come up easily, replace the top sheet of waxed paper with a clean piece, carefully turn the whole thing over, and peel off the waxed paper that's now on top. It should be easier to pick up cut-out cookies with your fingers or a thin spatula to place on the cookie sheet.

Grandma Clayton's Sand Tarts

MAKES ABOUT 3 1/2 DOZEN

●

Just as my maternal grandmother Nama was known for her Lemon Love Notes, my father's mother, Grandma, was known for her Sand Tarts. These cookies are not difficult to make, and always delicious! *(Photo, page 253)*

2 cups flour
¼ teaspoon salt
1½ cups powdered sugar, divided
½ pound butter, softened
1 teaspoon vanilla
½ cup chopped pecans

Preheat oven to 375 degrees. Lightly grease two large cookie sheets.

In a large mixing bowl, sift together the flour, salt and 1/2 cup of the sugar twice. Set aside.

Using an electric mixer with the paddle attachment, beat together the butter and vanilla just until the butter is soft. With the machine on low, slowly add the flour mixture, beating until incorporated and the dough is starting to hold together. Stir in chopped pecans. Using a small spring-release ice cream scoop (around 1 inch in diameter), scoop the dough into balls, pressing down to ensure the dough is staying together, and place around 1 inch apart on the prepared cookie sheets. Bake about 12 to 15 minutes or until just lightly brown. Cool slightly on cookie sheet, then roll in remaining 1 cup of powdered sugar. Store in an airtight container at room temperature.

NOTE If you don't have a paddle attachment for your electric mixer, work the butter and vanilla into the flour mixture by hand until all the flour is incorporated (this is how Grandma did it!). Also, in dry climates such as Colorado and Arizona, reduce the flour slightly, by about 2 tablespoons, if the batter seems too dry.

Kentucky Colonels

MAKES AROUND 2 DOZEN

●

Another long-standing Lee family recipe from my grandmother Nama, that includes the favored family ingredient—bourbon. Note that you need to start making these the day before.

¼ pound butter, softened
16 ounces powdered sugar (or more if needed)
4 to 6 tablespoons of good quality bourbon
Toasted pecan halves
4 squares unsweetened chocolate
2 squared semisweet chocolate

With an electric mixer using a whisk attachment, cream together the butter and sugar until fluffy and pale yellow. Mix in the bourbon until well blended. If needed, add more sugar to thicken. Refrigerate overnight.

The next day, using a small (1-inch) spring-loaded ice cream scoop, scoop the dough into balls. Insert a pecan half into each ball (break pecans in half if too large to fit). Refrigerate for 3 to 4 hours.

In the top of a double boiler over low heat (water at a low boil), melt the chocolate. Remove from heat. Using a fork, dip candy balls into the chocolate. Place on waxed paper to cool. Store covered in the refrigerator.

MAKE AHEAD Colonels will keep in the refrigerator for up to 1 week.

Chocolate Coconut Pecan Bars

MAKES AROUND 2 DOZEN

●

When we were in college, my roommate Cynthia's stepmother, Kathy, used to make these for us, and we couldn't stay away from them. As you'll discover, they are completely addictive! *(Photo, page 253)*

2 cups crushed cornflakes
3 tablespoons sugar
½ cup butter, melted
1 cup semisweet chocolate chips
1½ cups shredded coconut
1 cup chopped pecans
1 can (14 ounce) sweetened
   condensed milk

Preheat oven to 350 degrees. Lightly spray a 7x11-inch pan with nonstick cooking spray.

In a medium mixing bowl, mix together the cornflakes, sugar and melted butter (I usually use my hands). Press into the bottom of the prepared pan. Sprinkle chocolate chips evenly over the top. Sprinkle coconut over chips, and chopped pecans over the coconut. Drizzle milk evenly over all. Let it sink in for a few minutes, then bake for 30 to 35 minutes. Cool in the pan on wire rack, then cut in to bars. Store in an airtight container at room temperature.

Almond Macaroons

MAKES ABOUT 40

●

Mom was famous for her macaroons. Our good friend Katey Hartwell is especially fond of these treats.

1 cup (8 ounces) almond paste*
1 cup powdered sugar
2 large egg whites at room
   temperature
Dash salt
½ teaspoon vanilla
granulated sugar

** Available in most grocery stores
in 8-ounce cans.*

Preheat oven to 325 degrees. Grease and flour two large cookie sheets.

Chop the almond paste and place in a medium mixing bowl. Add the sugar and work with your fingers until blended. Add the egg whites, one at a time, blending well after each addition. Stir in the salt and vanilla. Drop dough with a spoon into individual pieces the size of a quarter onto prepared cookie sheets. Sprinkle with granulated sugar and bake for 20 minutes. Cool for a few minutes on the cookie sheet, then remove to a wire rack to cool completely. Store in an airtight container at room temperature.

Sally's Chocolate Almond Toffee

MAKES ABOUT 2 POUNDS

●

Mom was famous for her toffee. From the time I was a little girl, I remember there always being a coffee can full of toffee in our refrigerator. The tricky part of this recipe is getting the chocolate to adhere to the buttery toffee; using parchment paper and weighting it down as directed seems to work the best.

1 cup slivered almonds
1 cup ground almonds
1 cup butter
1⅓ cups sugar
3 tablespoons water
1 tablespoon light Karo syrup
8 ounces Hershey's milk chocolate, broken into pieces

Preheat oven to 350 degrees. Make a 9x11-inch rectangle with 1/2-inch sides out of parchment paper. (I staple the corners to keep the sides in place.) Place on a cookie sheet.

Place slivered almonds in a rimmed cookie sheet large enough to hold them in one layer. Place ground almonds in a separate rimmed cookie sheet. Toast both for around 8 to 10 minutes or until lightly browned, stirring occasionally. Watch carefully so they don't burn. Set aside.

In a large nonstick saucepan, melt the butter over medium heat. Stir in the sugar, water and Karo syrup. Keep stirring until the sugar is dissolved (the butter will be fully incorporated). Stop stirring, put a candy thermometer into the pan, keep the heat at medium, bring the mixture to a boil and cook until the temperature reaches 300 degrees (288 degrees if at high altitude). Stir infrequently—once around 245 degrees and again around 270 degrees. Watch it carefully once the temperature goes above 250 degrees as it can start to heat quickly at this point. Remove from heat, quickly stir in slivered almonds and immediately pour mixture into prepared pan. Using the back of a large wooden spoon, spread the mixture out to the edges of the paper pan, in an even layer. Set aside to cool to lukewarm.

While the candy is cooling, melt the chocolate in the top of a double boiler. Gently rub the top of the candy with a paper towel to soak up any excess grease. Spread evenly with half of the chocolate mixture. Sprinkle with 1/2 cup of the ground almonds. Tear the corners of the parchment paper so it lies flat. Cover the candy with wax paper and then a wooden cutting board to weight it down for around 5 minutes. Holding onto the cutting board and candy together, carefully turn them over. Remove the parchment paper, rub the top dry with a paper towel, and spread with remaining chocolate. Sprinkle with remaining 1/2 cup ground almonds. Cover with wax paper, then another cutting board or other flat surface that covers the candy. Place something very heavy on top, such as an iron muffin tin or large cookbook. This weighting down helps the chocolate adhere to the candy. Let sit at room temperature for 30 to 45 minutes, then place in the refrigerator until the chocolate hardens. Break into pieces and place in decorative candy boxes or bowls. Keeps best if stored in the refrigerator.

menus

Traditional Clayton Family Entertaining Dinner

Growing up, this was a menu that Mom often served, even if it meant some guests were treated to the same dishes more than once. Each dish is delicious and Mom always received rave reviews every time.

Camembert Sauté *p. 22*

Grilled Flank Steak with Mom's Steak and Lamb Marinade *p. 111*

Kentucky Corn Pudding *p. 198*

Red Leaf Lettuce with Hot Bacon Dressing *p. 69*

Nama's Rolls *p. 218*

Lemon Almond Ice Cream in Sally's Pecan Cookie Cups with Fresh Berries *p. 248*

●

Ladies' Brunch and Book Exchange

One year I came up with the idea of having a ladies' brunch that included a book exchange. Everyone brought a new or used book that they recommended and chose a different book to take home. It was a huge hit!

Cinnamon Raisin Bread Custard with Fresh Berries *p. 38*

Sausage, Mushroom and Pepper Strata *p. 35*

Caribbean Fruit Salad *(seasonedkitchen.com)*

Very Lemony Bread *p. 44*

Rhubarb Nut Bread *p. 45*

Pumpkin Cream Cheese Muffins *p. 41*

Blueberry Lemon Muffins *p. 42*

Chocolate Coconut Pecan Bars *p. 258*

Nama's Lemon Love Notes *p. 252*

Katharine Hepburn's Brownies *(seasonedkitchen.com)*

menus

Comfort-Food Snowy Day Dinner

When the snow flies and the temperature drops below freezing, there is nothing better than a warm, hearty meal featuring Mom's Veal Stroganoff and Captain Lee's Kentucky Bourbon Apple Pie! A snifter of brandy or glass of dessert wine in front of a fire completes a perfect evening.

Hearts of Palm Dip *(seasonedkitchen.com)* or Santo's Cheese Spread *p. 25*

Veal Stroganoff *p. 113*

Roasted Tomato and Arugula Salad *p. 71*

Herb Quick Bread *p. 217*

Captain Lee's Kentucky Bourbon Apple Pie *p. 228*

•

Summer BBQ

Summer menus are fun to plan because the grill often takes center stage. Dad loved lamb and he enjoyed it as a part of a Father's Day celebration. This menu's lamb and vegetable packets are grill-ready.

Sally's Smoked Trout Paté *p. 21*

Artichoke and Olive Salad with Lemon Dressing *(seasonedkitchen.com)*

or Carrot and Zucchini Soup *p. 56*

Barbequed Lamb Chops *p. 122*

Grilled Vegetable Packets *p. 201*

Parmesan-Buttermilk Cornbread *p. 219*

Aunt DeeDee's Cheesecake *p. 244*

Casual Fall Get-Together

*I like to serve this menu around Halloween as the perfect way to usher
in cooler weather. To save on time, make the pie in September
when peaches are at their peak and follow our directions for freezing.*

Melted Gruyère and Bacon Dip *p. 26*

Tomato Basil Bisque *p. 57*

Fall-Off-the-Bone Slow Cooker Short Ribs *p. 120*

Creamy Parmesan Polenta *p. 215*

Cilantro Peanut Coleslaw *p. 70*

Palisade Peach Pie or Apple Cake *p. 224, p. 237*

●

Family Thanksgiving Dinner

*In the Clayton household, Thanksgiving always meant lots of family and food! Mom was
renowned for her Apple-Sausage Stuffing, as I have become for my Fluffy Pumpkin Pie.
This menu provides updated versions for several Thanksgiving classics, including
creamed onions (Leek Gratin), candied sweet potatoes (Sausage, Yam
and Butternut Squash Casserole), and a new twist on a green bean casserole.*

Cheddar Chutney Tarts *p. 15*

Spinach and Goat Cheese Salad *p. 64*

Oven Roasted Turkey with Apple-Sausage Stuffing *p. 104*

Leek Gratin *p. 199*

Sausage, Yam and Butternut Squash Casserole *p. 200*

A Slightly Different Green Bean Casserole *(seasonedkitchen.com)*

Roasted New Potatoes (omitting the truffle oil) *p. 205*

Nama's Rolls *p. 218*

Fluffy Pumpkin Pie *p. 230*

Kim and Jan's Pecan Pie *p. 232*

index *Italicized page numbers indicate photos*